F.E.A.R

Hussain Abdullah

F.E.A.R may be purchased at special quantity discounts. Resale opportunities are available for donor programs, fund raising, book clubs, or other educational purposes for schools. For more information contact: FEARworkshop@gmail.com

ISBN (Paperback): 978-0-578-78614-8
ISBN (EBook): 978-0-578-78615-5
Author: Hussain Abdullah

Edited by: Shonda M. Curb, Shirley D. LaTour
Interior Design by Shirley D. LaTour

Publishing Consultant: Shirley D. LaTour of SL Elite Publishing, an assumed name of Shirley LaTour Enterprises, LLC
www.slelitepublishing.com

To my Mount Rushmore,
Angelina, Iris, Mary and Yusef

CONTENTS

PREFACE

When I decided to write this book, I wanted to chronicle and highlight critical moments and stories from my life that changed who I was as a person. Instead of focusing on the positive or negative aspects of the event, this prose is the "aha moment": 1) the instances in my life, personally or professionally, where a paradigm shift in my beliefs and behaviors have taken place; 2) the critical highlights that are often replayed over and over again as I make an everyday decision or a significant life-altering commitment or refusal.

These "resets" of my being have been put together as a handbook for your success. These accounts have been thoughtfully cultivated for your benefit to be used when necessary, similar to that of a hammer or a wrench. Used properly each lesson can turn a hardship into a handshake instead of headaches and heartbreak. In time, mastery will ultimately guide you along your path of prosperity in all that you strive to achieve.

I am honored that you have chosen to share in some of the significant memories from my life. In exchange for your time, I hope to share knowledge that allows you to "Forget Everything And Reset" (F.E.A.R).

INTRODUCTION

Isaiah 43:1, "Fear not: for I have redeemed thee, I have called thee by thy name; thou art mine".

What is fear? If you asked Merriam and Webster they would define fear as a noun, "an unpleasant often strong emotion caused by anticipation or awareness of danger" or as a transitive verb, "to be afraid of: expect with alarm." Lexico (lexico.com) defines fear as, "An unpleasant emotion caused by the belief that someone or something is dangerous, likely to cause pain, or a threat."

In the King James Version of the Bible, Isaiah 43:1 "Fear not: for I have redeemed thee, I have called thee by thy name; thou art mine."

The American Psychological Association (APA) describes fear and its physiological impacts on the body:

a basic, intense emotion aroused by the detection of imminent threat, involving an immediate alarm reaction that mobilizes the organism by triggering a set of physiological changes. These include rapid heartbeat, redirection of blood flow away from the periphery toward the gut, tensing of the muscles, and a general mobilization of the organism to take action (see fear response; fight-or-flight response).

In each of these definitions, there are similarities and subtle differences. The important takeaway is that fear is as real as you make it. To someone who is afraid, that fear can be debilitating and excruciating. The good news is fear can be controlled.

In the first definition by Merriam-Webster they select the phrase, "anticipation or awareness of danger" as a key to fear. Anticipation or awareness of danger is not a fixed object or idea that is set in stone.

"Anticipation or awareness of danger" certainly varies from person to person. An infant doesn't naturally fear fire. We can all agree that fire can be harmful to that infant and ourselves, yet he is unaffected by the mere presence of the flame.

When Lexico defines fear as "an unpleasant emotion", it is clearly stating the concept of a range of ideas associated with fear. As we age we associate concepts and what we deem as appropriate emotional responses to those situations or stimuli. The emotional responses to the same situations can vary by culture, age, gender, and personal experience.

Let's take the concept of abortion for example. This is a hot-button issue, it is highly debated and no matter where you stand on the topic you just had an emotional response when you read the previous sentence. Some of you might have experienced something that looks like or is defined as fear when reading it.

My purpose in mentioning a controversial idea was to get an emotional response from you and to prove that in an instant your emotions can change. If you can realize that emotions are ever-changing and under your control, you can use that knowledge to mold your responses to any circumstance.

Again, we find that even in psychology, the notion of fear is an, "intense emotion aroused by the detection of imminent threat". The point is overall, we can define fear. It might look different to different people as some of us are afraid of heights (acrophobia), water (aquaphobia), or even mathematics (arithmophobia).

The great thing about fear is, if in fact we can define it, we can control it. If fear looks different to different people, we cannot say that fear is the same thing to all people. If fear is an emotion, we can learn how to manage it and how it impacts us physically, philosophically, and financially.

People fear the unknown or what they don't understand. There are large masses of people who are afraid to invest because of the unknown. You might have little to no knowledge of real estate or investing. After reading this book you will have a new or more developed sense of real estate, investing, fear, and finance.

1

VANITY

"I use to think Jordan's and a gold chain was living it up."
Nas

Back at the crib

2003

There is a popular saying that it is better to have had love and lost it then to never have had love at all (Alfred Lord Tennyson). It's poetic and depending on who you ask it might even be factual. Like all things, it's a matter of perspective. There is something to be said for the thrill of the hunt. Oftentimes, the chase is more exciting than the catch.

Growing up in the inner city of one of the world's largest and most competitive cities you learn fast that to survive you have to stand out. As a kid from Brooklyn standing out meant one thing: being dressed to impress. From an early age, I was taught that presentation meant a lot.

Being born in the spring of 1982, a time known as the unofficial birth of Air Jordan and a cultural revolution that began to place a relatively new genre of music called rap, the hip hop culture played a major role in my evolution and how I would see myself growing up.

It was a time that saw the rise of the crack epidemic. The Dinkins years. The rise of young black men making money and making sure to show it. Oversized gold chains with custom pendants, customized high-end European outfits with customized European vehicles to match. Rakim and Big Daddy Kane, amongst others, portraying the image of a lifestyle anyone would aspire to.

As a child it all seems normal. You see what you see when you watch TV. You learn what cool is. As amazing as some of the imagery might have looked on other rap videos, it's not very realistic to have a 30-millimeter gold rope chain and a custom high-end tracksuit.

Even now in 2020, some things just look better on TV. As time progresses, we hit the early nineties and cool shifts. At the time other trendsetters in fashion and in hip-hop began to rise in popularity.

Knowledge of self and a pro-African sentiment became the norm with groups like: A Tribe Called Quest, X-Clan, Queen Latifah, and others. One notable artist was Grand Puba of the rap group Brand Nubians. His style was more accessible. He wore clothes that everyday people would wear: jeans and rugby's, a hoodie, and a book bag. He was a kid. Someone you could emulate.

As a young boy, I was always spoken to and treated as a young king in fact, I was named after one, King Hussein bin Tal of Jordan. In the Arabic language, the name "Hussain" translates to beautiful or handsome. I was also affectionately called "The Golden Child", named after a character in a popular 1980's Eddie Murphy film.

Confidence was not lacking in my upbringing, or was it? I remember going to stores with my mom and shopping out of boxes and off of racks in overpacked stores on Fifth Avenue in Brooklyn. If you're from the area, you know the name Mike's. What I didn't know at the time was that Mike's was a second-hand clothing store. But I did remember the brand names. I remember Benetton, Girbaud, Guess, and the highest of heights, Polo.

· · ·

I CAN'T THINK of anything better at the time than having a new outfit made up of Girbaud jeans, a Polo shirt, and a pair of Nike's. Similar to the iconic red tab on a pair of Levi's jeans, Girbaud had a signature placement of their name on the front of jeans on the outside flap of their pants that covers the zipper and button of the jeans. It was a small, one inch by a half an inch patch that you could miss very easily. At that time, teens who were in "the know", knew them and knew where to look.

Happy Holidays

1989

I can distinctly remember one time. It was me, around my tenth birthday. My mom took me to Mike's and it happened. I found a pair of Girbaud jeans. These were even cooler than the regular pair with the navy-blue patch. I happened to find a pair with the patch that was made out of denim (records scratch, rockets blast, a woman faints).

I've heard my older brother talk about these. These were the ones Grand Puba had. The only thing that made getting these jeans better than anything else was that my brother wanted them and he didn't have them. When I came home with them I showed him and he was like, "The denim stitch? Man, how?" It was the stamp of approval. I knew what cool was. For a day or two, it was a stamp of approval.

Now, to make sure you understand just one more small detail about these jeans, my classmates and friends also knew about these jeans because they also had older siblings. Some even went to school with my older brother. These were a big deal. You also have to remember they came from Mike's.

I want to say my mom paid $4 for them. They had a small ink spot on them (I'll explain that in detail later). Mike sold used and damaged clothes. There would have been no other way my mom could have afforded and/or even thought to buy me something as costly as a pair of Girbaud jeans at the time. Fate was on my side.

Girbaud Jeans
1992

My brother was sixteen at the time, so I had an advantage that he might not have had. I benefited from and experienced everything vicariously through him. I looked up to him. He was popular. He was a barber and he was a stylish (and still is) guy.

If you've ever watched the movie *Juice*, the breakout role of now-deceased rapper Tupac Shakur, you might recall a scene where Omar Epps' character "Q" is getting dressed for school. Q puts on a mini fashion show changing outfits with different combinations of hats, footwear, and accessories before his little brother approves and he leaves his apartment. That was us.

Around the age of fourteen, my brother pierced his ear. I remember it well. He used ice to numb his lobe; then he used the stove to heat up and sterilize a needle that had a white thread on it.

He had a wooden brush that he used to serve as a firm surface to hold his ear in place as he pushed the needle into his left ear. I thought it was the coolest thing in the world. This guy just performed surgery on himself and he had a gold hoop in his ear.

I did what any "Golden Child" would do, I asked my mom if I could get my ear pierced too. The best thing about being the baby in the house was, he got in trouble for piercing his ear and I got to go to a jewelry store with my mom and have my ear pierced with her. It was perfect.

The days of emulating my big brother had become more obvious than ever. This included wearing his clothes, cologne, we called them oils (Musk, blue Nile, etc.); five dollar bottles you could get from street vendors (again this book is meant to paint a picture of Brooklyn the way it used to be. If you weren't there, sorry you missed it). Finishing off a shopping trip by spending your last five dollars at the oils' spot was great.

When we got a bit older the pattern continued. My brother got his first tattoo. He had to hide his tattoo. He was about 18 or 19. About a year later I got my first tattoo. I know tattoos are everywhere now and young people are getting them all over. Back in the mid-90s having a tattoo was a big deal.

Stars like Tupac, Allen Iverson, and Dennis Rodman were demonized for their "excessive work". If you compared their tattoos to a local high schooler in any city you'd be hard pressed to see a difference. In certain ways having an older brother protected me, in other ways, it sped up my development, personal style, and flare.

Being stylish and well-dressed was a trend that started with my grandfather, "Negrete" (neh-gre-tay), a nickname rooted in the Spanish word for black, "negro", which he was given because of his darker skin tone. Negrete was always sharp.

A short, thin, Puerto Rican man that somehow always captivated a room when he entered. He passed away when I was very young but I always remember him having a fresh shave, his hair was always well kept, and he always wore suits and jewelry.

He was known for having large amounts of cash and being well respected in the community. This tradition would be passed from Negrete to my father and again passed down to us. As a young boy, I have memories of my father taking me to Juma, (think Sunday mass for Christians, except Friday's are the day of worship for Muslims) and rubbing oils on me.

Negrete

1960's

I REMEMBER in sixth grade a classmate of mine had a birthday party. Her older sister had on the coolest sneakers I had ever seen. They were white, red, and grey with two diagonal crisscross straps. They would come to be known as the Bugs Bunny 8s. These were Nike Air Jordan's.

They looked perfect. By chance, I also had a pair of black and grey Nike's with two diagonal crisscross straps. They were Nike Air Raids. I liked them because I liked them. I wasn't brainwashed just yet.

A couple of weeks would go by, and I would go with my mom and brother to visit family in Staten Island, and there they were again! My cousin had the same sneakers. They were everywhere. I never really cared about sneakers that much until that point. And then it began. I was on the hunt for my first pair of Air Jordan's.

I begged my mother for a pair. My mother didn't have money for a pair of $100 sneakers. To add insult to injury, my foot was a size 6; that meant I couldn't buy sneakers and pay children's prices any longer. My Nike Air Raids were a size 5.5, they cost about $65. That $100 price tag was a huge jump. But Ma being Ma she tried to make it happen. She said we can go in a few days (payday).

It was a Saturday filled with trips to different sneaker stores. The day ended with stops on the famed Flatbush Avenue. If you've never heard of Flatbush

Avenue in Brooklyn think of what Harlem means to fashion in Manhattan. That is what Flatbush is to Brooklynites. We ended up at a store called Ragga Muffin. At the time, it was a sneaker store that we frequented because we were able to haggle a bit. The search felt endless but it wasn't fruitless.

I didn't find the sneakers I sought. They were sold out everywhere. Back in the days before the internet and the aftermarket sneaker sales industry you could get a pair of sneakers a week or two after they had come out.

They were expensive but they were accessible. People didn't stand in lines for sneakers. I was heartbroken until I saw something even better than the sneakers my friend's sister and my cousin had.

They were black with teal and purple and they also had two diagonal crisscross straps. They were the new Nike Air Jordan 8s!! At the time I had no idea. I'd learn more about them later, but at the time they were the best sneakers I had ever laid eyes on with a price tag of $110. Good job haggling Ma. The retail price for these sneakers was $125. Thank goodness they were black. I couldn't see my mom paying that price for white sneakers that I was going to use to play outside.

I remember the feeling I had when I got to one of my other cousin's houses a few blocks away. "Not, Hus with the new Jordan's!" Yup, that was me. I couldn't wait to wear them to school. I felt like a million bucks.

Yup, these are the new ones, I shared as if I (my mom) purchased them with that knowledge.

Things were perfect until another classmate and friend would enter the classroom with a pair of black, red and white sneakers with diagonally crossing straps. How could she? How could they? What was going on? At the time (again, I couldn't know the significance at the time) Michael Jordan and the Bulls were wrapping up their third consecutive championship run known as a "Three-Peat". He was at the height of his career and the sports world in general.

Nike would capitalize on this by making multiple colorways of the same shoe to maximize sales. The white pair were the preseason release, the aqua pair were sold during the regular season, and the version with the red and white went on sale for the NBA's postseason. My birthday was at the end of March. The playoffs begin in mid-April. These sneaker release dates also lined up with back to school, Christmas, and Easter. Nike learned quickly when to drop new items.

Around this time in the late '80s and early '90s, there was also another trend on the rise. The only thing hotter than Jordan's in New York City was Ralph Lauren's Polo. This was also the height of the crack (cocaine) epidemic.

With this new wave of crime and addiction came tons of money and new ways to spend it. That also translated to more teens and young adults wanting to achieve this level of flash by any means necessary.

The advent of "wilding" is a term that became infamous in the city with the case of the now "Exonerated 5" and then known as the "Central Park 5". Wilding was when a group of male teens usually black and brown but also white went out in packs and terrorized the city. One group was famous for a niche target, the "Lo-Life's". "Lo", short for Polo, was a play on words because by definition they were criminals (lowlifes); see Thirstin Howl the 3rd (the most famous of the Lo-Life's).

They would swarm high-end boutiques and steal racks of clothes. It was called racking up (see Rack-Lo another famous Lo-Life). One of the most popular marks was the Polo Mansion. It is a huge dwelling with a restaurant and a store inside of it located in Manhattan.

The Lo Mansion was the creme de la creme of "boosting" (stealing). They had Ralph Lauren everything, spoons, teacups, couches, and drapes. It was a home where every nook and cranny was designed by Ralph himself. They had the most exclusive items which meant the highest prices.

This was the late '80s and early '90s. Polo had sweaters and jackets with price tags in the $400 to $500 range. I write "had" because they didn't hold on to them for long. Those items were stolen off the racks instantly.

Boosters would run into a store 20 to 30 deep (people), grab as much as they could, and run out of the stores.

The crime sprees got so ridiculous the advent of a concept called "stacking" became cool. Stacking was when you would wear one piece (as in a piece of clothing) underneath another piece, on top of another piece, underneath another one etcetera. Socks, underwear, headbands, scarfs you name it. It was about showing off.

Ralph Lauren used to print the same images on different clothing items. For example, he would lay out his latest line on his famed Polo Bears (which later became re-popularized by Kanye West). To this day I still have my RL2000 Bear set which included a red t-shirt, long sleeve button up, a crew neck sweater, a wool knit sweater and a baseball cap.

The set is red and the bear is dressed in all black with grey ski's. The perfect color combination to wear with, you guessed it: Chicago Bulls inspired Nike Air Jordan's. We are talking about a couple of thousand dollars' worth of clothes.

Remember at the time boosting was at its peak when I was in grammar school. I won't say any names but there were some folks several years older than I, who had a whole lot of Polo and did a whole lot of stacking and if my memory serves me well did not have $400 per shirt money.

. . .

I WILL ALSO ADD the RL2000 Bear came out in 1992 one of the most popular years for collecting as it was an Olympic year. '88, '92, '96 were the golden age of Polo collecting. I will say the 2000 Bear was my favorite because my brother had that bear (amongst others).

My crew neck was actually his from back in 1992. The other additional items were retrieved later on via trade or aftermarket purchase. Another note, I also still own a '92 Big Ski turtleneck. It was passed down from one generation (stolen) to another generation. I ended up with it by trading for it.

The original story goes: a kid by the name of "SKI", my senior by about 10 years, boosted it because it had his name on it. The price tag was about $375 back in 1992. One of my family members obtained it and the rest is history. I never traded or sold it because of the sentimental value it had and it was red so I could wear it with...

Now that you have the back story and the evolution of my desire to dress to impress we can move on to when the opportunity came to really shine (my perception at the time). High school is when you begin to really come into your own. You can work (although my first paying job was in fifth grade at 10 years old) and spend your own money on what you want.

. . .

THE STAKES HAD RISEN and so had a new trend in hip hop. As the crack era went away a new form of rapper emerged, the "post drug dealer". Artists like Raekwon and Ghostface Killah of the Wu-Tang Clan and most notably Jay-Z made songs about the lavish life they lived based on the narcotics they sold in a past life.

The Big Ski - 7th grade
1994

They set the bar extremely high. I remember going to Kings Plaza mall every week to buy something. My mother could only spend so much. Freshman year it was Tommy Hilfiger, sophomore and junior year it was Polo, Polo, and more Polo. With senior year came new fashion.

That year Polo didn't cut it. Jay-Z made Iceberg famous. At the time Iceberg had a line called "History". They partnered with the likes of Warner Brothers and other iconic figures to create high-end products. I remember being 17 spending $1,000 on a sweatsuit (I still have the tags). $300 on pants and so on.

$1,000 sweat suit

2001

It was a high for me. The attention was an adrenaline rush. Let's go back for a second. Remember earlier in the chapter when I explained my Girbaud jeans had an ink stain on them. Let's discuss that for a moment.

When boosting was at its peak they tried to slow that down with alarms. One of the types of alarms was plastic and they were filled with ink. If you didn't have the key to slide it off properly the ink would spill out and render the garment worthless. Boosters created ways to circumvent that deterrent but from time to time someone would slip up and ink would inevitably make it on a clothing item.

Boosters stole all types of clothing; ink spots on your clothes were almost a badge that you were a part of that circle. Switching tags was also popular. If you were crafty enough you could slide a price tag off of let's say a $500 item and if you weren't greedy you could swap that with a $150 tag and with the right cashier you would walk out as if no crime had taken place.

Other times certain items such as socks or under-wear didn't have sophisticated anti-theft devices on them so you would see people stacking socks. Three pairs of $50 socks just to say look at me I have $150 worth of socks on at one time.

At one point in high school, my thirst for that atten-tion got to the point where I would buy new sneakers just to say I bought new sneakers. Sometimes a new pair of Jordan's would come out and I had to make sure I had them or I felt like my stock would fall.

I remember buying a pair of Jordan 15s two sizes too big just to have them at school the following Monday. Jordan's were released on Saturday's; Nike made sure to maximize their release dates as always.

· · ·

BY THIS TIME the lines and pre-orders had begun. My regular sneaker stores were sold out; I had to do what I had to do. I had so many pairs of sneakers that I didn't wear; it was almost embarrassing. I even began to buy the same exact sneaker twice so I could have a pair for games and a pair for wearing outside. I would show up to a basketball game with shoes around my neck and the matching pair on my feet.

There were some kids who couldn't afford a pair of Jordan's. Imagine how it made me feel as a poor kid (at the time I had no idea) to have two brand new pairs on at the same time. The stacking culture was real. And I embraced it.

I had matching book bags and hats, jackets, scarf and glove sets, and all sorts of accessories. I would even switch up jewelry items. At the time I was wearing diamond rings, gold, Gucci chains, and Cuban links to school when other students weren't wearing jewelry at all.

The only other student at my school who was able to keep up with my level of frivolous spending was a student one year my senior. He had a diamond cross and a Cuban link. He would wear leather Avirex jackets and Coogi outfits in rotation. It was a daily fashion show. We would nod in respect to one another. It was a competition.

· · ·

HE WOULD WEAR something really eye-catching and I had to one-up it. I would come to school with a new piece and he would give me that look like this isn't over. We went back and forth until he dropped out. This student was also a known drug dealer with two older brothers who also sold drugs. He would wear their clothes to keep up the charade.

This pattern continued even after high school. As I mentioned earlier, Minneapolis was an eye-opening experience. I remember my first night in the new city. I had no idea I would be living in a house during my time in the Midwest. I didn't know anyone with a driveway or a real backyard. It felt like a whole new world. It was a culture shock.

I remember how I felt when I first got to the town. I stuck out like a sore thumb. The music was different, the way people dressed was different. There was one instance where I was on a bus coming from the Mall of America and there was a group of kids on the back of the bus and we started speaking. These guys were probably local celebrities of sorts as far as teenage popularity goes.

In my eyes they looked ridiculous. They had on Lugz boots, silver chains, fake diamond stud earrings, Fubu, and Eckō. All of these things were no-nos in New York City. Timberlands were the standard and still are in the city.

Those clothing labels were not acceptable and I would never wear a piece of silver or any imitation jewelry. I hate knock offs and bootlegged items. The fake it 'til you make it mentality was not and is not one I support or am fond of.

To these guys and other guys all around the city, this was the standard. The best part of this situation was, to them I looked ridiculous. I was wearing a Ralph Lauren Polo teddy bear shirt, Girbaud jeans and Jordan's with a fitted baseball cap with several pieces of gold jewelry.

One of the guys on the back of the bus actually made fun of my shirt. He said something to the effect of, "Why would a man wear a shirt with a bear on it?"

At the time I was shocked at the audacity. My shorts cost more than their jewelry. It wasn't even expensive silver, it was middle of the mall jewelry. They thought my jewelry wasn't real. It was appalling. This was one of many situations where it was obvious I wasn't a local.

None of it made sense to me. Being from Brooklyn, the idea was to dress to impress. Who would be impressed with $30 t-shirts from the mall that everyone else had? What I didn't realize at the time was that malls were all they had in places like Minneapolis. I wouldn't play basketball in those clothes back home. I would have to explain why I had them in the first place.

This mindset continued for a short while longer. I remember one week where I flew out to the city as I did every few weeks specifically to buy a Cuban link and a Jesus piece. This item was the one the Notorious B.I.G rapped about. The most popular rap artists out at the time had them and I was finally going to get mine.

Imagine the mindset of someone who was willing to take a trip, purchase airfare, and fly halfway across the country to go shopping. At the time it was one of the coolest things I had ever done. I felt like a millionaire. At that point I was doing better financially then I had ever imagined.

This piece was an 8mm thick, 26-inch-long Cuban link necklace that weighed 242 grams of 14kt gold (including the pendant); that is almost a half a pound of gold. The piece also had two 10-point diamonds (one in each eye) and about 30 3-point diamonds in the crown of thorns on the pendant.

This wasn't a small or cheap piece of jewelry at all. I remember getting cramps in my neck and back after wearing that and the smaller Jesus piece and figure chain I wore at the same time.

That trip cost me close to $6,000, and I didn't even feel it. I had more in the bank and my 401k so it didn't bother me one bit. That piece was a status symbol. It meant the world to me at the time and little did I know worlds were about to collide soon thereafter.

During my time in the Midwest, I had several older friends. I worked for a Fortune 500 company in a call center in what was Minneapolis' version of Wall Street. I was one of maybe two or three other teens that worked at this office. Most of the other employees were middle-aged.

I had a lot of work moms that made sure I was taken care of since everyone knew I was out there pretty much by myself. They were always concerned with the way I carried myself as far as walking around wearing expensive items and carrying large amounts of cash in a tough area, as well as commuting on public transportation.

I would go shopping during my lunch break and come back with $400 Coogi sweaters or $150 sneakers. I never ate lunch on my break; I always ordered in. I liked to hang out during my break. In hindsight, they were all correct. My teenage invincibility complex was definitely a factor.

In my mind, it was all normal. In Brooklyn no one had cars. Seeing people dressed nicely waiting for a bus or riding the train was a regular occurrence. In the Midwest, everyone had cars; only people who couldn't afford one used the bus system. It was a cultural shift I didn't really pay attention to at the time.

One day one of my friends we will call "Duck" saw me coming out of the elevator and coming onto the floor and he said, "Can I ask you a question?"

"Yea, what's up Duck?"

"How much did you spend on that outfit?"

"Over a thousand."

He then continued, "How much money do you have in your pocket?"

Duck caught me slippin' that day. Normally I would have a thousand or two in my pocket. Not on this day. That day I had maybe $20 in my pocket.

Now I knew I was making maximum contributions to my retirement plan and I knew I had money in the bank. I also knew Duck had a house and I rented an apartment (it was a nice apartment in the uptown area of Minneapolis, a few blocks from a lake). In addition, I was aware of the fact that Duck would pick me up and drop me off to the night gym he ran to play basketball.

Duck was a minimalist. He owned real estate and he saw how frivolous I was with my capital. So, I kept my mouth shut as I saw the point he was making when he exclaimed, "So you would rather have $1,000 worth of clothes and $20 in your pocket instead of the other way around?"

F.E.A.R instantly set in and I began to become more mindful about my spending habits. The fact was that it snows more than it doesn't in Minnesota. In waist-deep snow, nothing stops. The city has skyways built into the downtown area. The skyway system is a second story set of walkways that connect the metropolis so you can get from one side of the financial district to the other without having to step foot outside.

Cold weather and snow do not stop the city from working. I also didn't wear my new sneakers in the snow. I worked 60-hour weeks plus Saturdays when they offered the opportunity to do so. I lived to work so there was no need to try and impress anyone.

As time went on I began to slow down on my extravagant purchases. I didn't stop buying sneakers. I was a collector. I had a system set up at Foot Locker where the manager would let me prepay for the sneakers that were coming out the next month and he would give me an accessory item with my sneakers because I was such a good customer.

I didn't wait in lines. I would even get my pair the day before the release. He would call me once the shipments came in so I could pick my pairs up without a hassle. It was amazing to walk around the mall on a Thursday with a pair of sneakers that didn't even come out yet.

I did however begin to take advantage of the five (5) for $20 sales the store offered. You could get five (5) plain t-shirts for $20. I would get different color shirts to match the new sneakers and I would shop at the Gap to get sweatpants and track pants.

I began to wear clothes that weren't so logo heavy and wore my jewelry less and less while focusing on adding to my quality of life. Everyone I knew owned a home. They paid a mortgage that was comparable to the rent I paid in my one-bedroom apartment and they had two to three times the space.

I began to take notice of the cars and boats my coworkers owned and saw that my focus was very small. The other key take away some of you might have missed during my recollection of the Polo bear story was that this situation took place on the back of a bus. I was 19 at the time. At that point with the income I was earning I should have been in a car not on the back of a bus with thousands of dollars in clothes and jewelry.

Here we are about 20 years later. I look back on that and think how much of a shame it was for us to behave that way. Imagine if we had positive role models around us who could show us about investing. What if trying to look like drug dealers or actually selling drugs or stealing clothes to seem as if we had money wasn't an aspiration?

I remember as a teen almost everyone thought I sold drugs. What else would someone think? I wore expensive jewelry, I had ridiculously expensive clothes every day. I always had wads of cash in my pocket. I flaunted it. People thinking I sold drugs was actually a compliment at that point. It was cool, at least the way it looked on television was.

It is interesting now when I see that I became Duck in a sense. On most days you will catch me in sweats and a t-shirt usually advertising one of my own businesses or one of my friends' businesses. I typically do not wear any jewelry; however, I travel frequently and live in a beautiful home in a wonderful and safe neighborhood.

I am blessed to only drive new cars, and I am fortunate enough to be able to give back to the communities that I invest in. I offer my time as a volunteer and a mentor. I also give donations and scholarships both privately and through my businesses.

Duck had it right, looking back we are at the parallel points in life. I am 38 now and he was then, without his notable commentary as well as his advice and mentorship throughout my time in the Midwest who knows what my fate would be now.

I wasn't wise enough to fully comprehend what Duck had intended to show me at the time but I was smart enough to take heed to his message: and, F.E.A.R allowed the evolution of my daily interactions to manifest into a better lifestyle. Consequently, a new set of values began to take precedence over shallower, less important items like clothing and fashion.

2

VALUE

"The greatest prison that people live in is the fear of
what other people think."
David Icke

Downtown Brooklyn

2015

Over 20 years later I look back on our previous choices and think how much of a shame it was for us to behave that way. In my defense, I wasn't all that bad. I didn't spend every dime I had on clothes and jewelry. I also worked and was an entrepreneur. I had a clothing business where I sold my clothes and also cut hair after school and on the weekends, when I wasn't playing basketball.

I always had drive and a sense that money meant something so I had to hold on to it. With some luck, I was even gifted a copy of the book that helped me to learn more about investing and F.E.A.R my spending habits. The book was Robert Kiyosaki's *Rich Dad, Poor Dad*.

This book led to my first Certificate of Deposit (CD) investment. A CD is a bank account where in exchange for lack of access to your funds, you gain larger (at that time - banks aren't paying anything on CDs nowadays) interest rates on your balance.

My first CDs were for $1,000 for 12 months at 5% and $5,000 for 6 months at 6% at age 19. I wanted to see how the process worked. I didn't need the funds at the time so I thought it best to make more than the 1% interest my regular savings account was earning.

Let's fast forward a bit. The year was 2015 and I had come into my own as an investor. I had just bought out Agita (more about Agita in Chapter Five), I had bought and sold a condo in Brooklyn and I had my three (or 2.5 as one condo was co-owned) condos in Houston. The deal with Agita for $50,000 had just come through and things were looking up. You have to try and imagine my feelings at the time.

. . .

IN A YEAR AND A HALF SPAN, I went from a
50/50 owner on one property to the owner of three and
a member of two different Limited Liability Corpora-
tions (LLCs). I had three separate days in my life where
I pocketed more money than the majority of American
families would gross in a year even now five years later.
The average person doesn't have $50,000 and $130,000
days especially not in the same year.

I was on a high. It was time to treat myself. I earned
it. My gross rental income exceeded my net earnings as
a teacher. I lived in a co-op apartment that was owned
outright, free and clear (I didn't have a mortgage). So
why not spend a little (more than I was accustomed to)?
Spend I did.

This wasn't the first time I had spent several thousand dollars in a day shopping. I've made several
multiple thousand-dollar jewelry purchases and a
handful of thousand-dollar shopping sprees on clothing
items or car accessories. I believed it was regular and, in
my experience, money comes and money goes. You can't
take it with you.

Within two weeks my $50,000 was closer to $5,000.
The key purchases or new additions to my lifestyle
included financing a 2013 BMW 5 series, an 18kt
yellow gold Presidential Rolex with a diamond dial and
bezel, a 1992 Polo Indian Head knit sweater (which I

still haven't worn outside of a photoshoot), and a slew of other relatively smaller purchases.

In some form of self-defense, I'd like to put my decisions in perspective. Let's start with the BMW. This vehicle was certified pre-owned by BMW. I had a 3-year warranty and it wasn't a seven (7) series. I figured I wanted a spacious luxury vehicle.

I could have sprung for the seven (7) but for one thing: Agita once told me you can't go from A to Z. Meaning, if I were to buy a seven (7) series, what was next? It was better to gradually build up so the novelty was still there during the ascension.

I could have financed or leased a new vehicle but I knew better about cars being depreciating liabilities. Why spend $75,000 on a car that I could spend $40,000 on? In my eyes I got the same vehicle for half price. It was still new, given most people drive vehicles older than 2-3-years-old.

I always drive new vehicles. The certainty of having a reliable vehicle is crucial for me. I also had a rule that my car had to be paid for by my investments. My car note was under $500 and with gas, car washes, and insurance (my maintenance was free for the first 3 years) the car cost about $900 a month. My net profit from rent at the time was around $1,200.

Next up the Indian head knit. I've always been a collector. It's something my mother instilled in me as a child early on. Earlier, in Chapter One, I went into lengthy details about the impact of the Lo-Life's and the cultural implications of having certain sought-after items. The Indian head knit was and still is one of the most highly coveted pieces of the collection.

As a teen, I could never get my hands on one. They were extremely rare. My brother Yus had one but it was either sold or traded during his high school years. My time as a collector was 1996-2000. I still have the commemorative Polo bears that were released at the time. Polo would release an artifact once a year to hall-mark a collection.

Buying this sweater was like my Rosebud for those of you familiar with Citizen Kane. It was something I window shopped for on eBay for years and now I would make sure it was mine. With price tags as high as $2,000 it was something I really had to make sure I felt like I could afford before bidding on it. I have never lost on a bid; it is part of my competitive nature.

I would bid ridiculous amounts on an item that caught my eye to ensure I was victorious. I still bid this way. I ended up bidding $1,500 on the sweater and winning it for about $800. To me, it was a steal at that price. It is still a trophy to me and it was worth every penny. In full transparency: If I didn't buy it then I'd still buy it now; it is that important to me.

. . .

THE LAST AND most important item on the list of the big three is the item I wanted the longest. The nickname alone says so much about the fine timepiece. The "Presidential" Rolex. The official name of this particular Rolex is a Day-Date; just in reference to the watch's day of the week and date of the month features on the dial.

The nickname was earned by the esteemed panel of owners over the years, Pablo Escobar, John F. Kennedy Jr., Dr. Martin Luther King Jr., Boris Yeltsin, Muammar al-Gaddafi amongst others, including a slew of other celebrities and entertainers. I first saw this watch in the mid-nineties. The retail price tag at that time was about $32,000.

The first time I had a serious thought about purchasing this watch was back in 2003. I spoke with my uncle about it and he said Hoobs, (a family nickname) "You're not ready for the Prezi. You don't live the lifestyle. That's a big boy watch." He asked me where I was going to purchase the watch?

I told him I could get one on Canal St. Canal St is in Chinatown in lower Manhattan. Canal St had a reputation for having, how should I put it gently, "slum" jewelry, also known as Gumby gold (because your neck could turn green just like the character's skin color).

My uncle was a savant when it came to all things high-end. He told me about Tourneau, amongst so many other lessons on a variety of subjects. The Big Ski turtleneck originally came from him. We were extremely close; in fact, we share the same birthday. His opinion was vital so the conversation ended there.

What makes this wristwatch so special? For starters, it is a solid 18k gold watch with a weight of about 8oz. To date, the technology in the watch can be duplicated and found in $32 watches. The then famous quickset feature allowed you to change the date without having to wind the watch 60 times to correct the date.

That feature was a game-changer back in the 1970s. The double quickset was even more revolutionary as you could correct the date and day by pulling the pin out either one-click or two clicks to correct your desired feature.

Before this advent, the wealthy and prestigious would have to sit and wind their watches for several minutes to keep accurate time. Rolex is also known for its accurate timekeeping, as the second hand doesn't tick, it rolls. Meaning it is accurate even down to the millisecond. It also has a kinetic feature that allows the watch to work for 40 hours without movement.

If you don't know what a watch winder is, allow me to explain. Most Rolex owners have more than one watch. If your watch isn't battery operated like a Rolex you would have to adjust your watch every time you wanted to wear it. A watch winder is a device that allows you to set your watch in a moving display case that keeps the timepiece in motion while you are not using it.

My first Presidential Rolex encounter was during my first attempt to purchase one in 2010. It was a boring Saturday morning. At the time I was renting an apartment in Brooklyn with my then girlfriend. I was browsing the net and I saw that Tourneau (the only licensed non-Rolex retailer in the nation) had the watch I wanted for $20,000.

I had to act quickly. This was the first time I saw the watch for under $28,000. I jumped up and headed to Fifth Avenue in Manhattan. This potential purchase led to an argument and a detour on my trip.

I just mentioned at the time I was renting an apartment with my girlfriend (ex-wife). It is kind of a hard sell to mention you're going out to purchase a $20,000 watch when your girlfriend isn't your fiancé. I saw her perspective and I had a decision to make. I think I played it well.

I called her brother and had him take a trip with me. First stop, Tourneau, second stop, Tiffany's. I really wanted my watch. Now before you pass judgment let's keep in perspective here that we can highlight the attributes of a successful entrepreneur with this story. I didn't give up. I found a way to make the deal happen. No, still judgmental? Oh well, I tried.

· · ·

WE GET to Tourneau and the watch isn't the one I wanted; it was a "unisex" version of the watch. It was a 24-millimeter version, basically a woman's watch. I needed the 36-millimeter version. The newer 44-millimeter option didn't exist until 2016.

I didn't want to leave empty-handed so I purchased a $10,000 Rolex Sea Dweller. It had a cool feature with a deployment clip on the bracelet. This allows for a sea diver to adjust the watch with the click of a button to widen it so it could fit on the outside of their diving suit in order to calculate their time and depth. I liked it. I didn't love it.

I also made a stop at Tiffany's and spent another $14,000 on a platinum and diamond solitaire ring. I'd like to remind you to focus on the important thing here. As an entrepreneur, I am willing to go above and beyond to make a deal work. Still no takers?

The point of this part of the story is I didn't love the watch so I rarely wore it. Because I rarely wore it I noticed it didn't keep time well. I thought I had been had. I went back to Tourneau and I was very upset.

"I spent $9,800 on a broken watch?" I asked. I settled for the watch because it was close enough to the other Rolex I wanted as of 1999: The Pepsi Rolex. Without getting too far into detail: the dial is black, the bezel is red and blue; hence the moniker.

· · ·

THE FIRST TIME I saw this watch, Brooklyn rapper M.E.M.P.H.I.S Bleek wore it during a music video he was featured in, "Hey Papi", starring Jay-Z. In 2001, I went to purchase the watch for $5,300. I wish I had. To date, you can't find one under $11,500.

I ended up getting a lesson in fine timepieces and also getting a 100% refund. Tourneau is the only non-Rolex store that sells 100% certified authentic Rolexes for a reason. Clients spend $100,000 in five minutes, and it's a regular purchase in a store like that. You have a guarantee that their watchmakers are certified to work on your watches, and that you are insured for their work. They do not sell any aftermarket items.

What that means is, if you were to change the dial or any part of your watch and it stopped working you would have to find a non-Rolex jeweler to repair it and it would be worth significantly less as it was an after-market item. This type of transaction could reduce your watch value by up to 80%.

If you are going to spend money on big ticket items you should know why. The last, and very important, reason made me comfortable with this purchase. This timekeeping device is also one of a few select brands that appreciates over time.

These items are actually an asset. This was an investment. It is as good as having money in the bank. To date, this watch is worth more than the BMW I purchased in 2015. If I were so inclined, I could sell the watch and sweater and be close to the $50,000 price tag all over again.

Typically, this type of exorbitant object is gifted. It's a token of 20 years of service or a retirement gift. To follow suit, the rear case is customarily engraved. I engraved my watch with the phrase, "Everything in time", as a reminder that with patience and discipline you can accomplish what you set out to realize.

To be clear I also didn't spend the whole $50,000 on shopping. I knew the benefits of financing items. I learned about the concept of "OPM" or other people's money, from another piece of literature I picked up in the early 2000's, "OPM". I invested about $15,000 to $20,000 in real estate and debt consolidation and removal (with the sole intention of reinvesting the lines of credit back into more real estate).

Hussain, where is all of this going? We have heard all about your shopping sprees and your high school fashion shows but what is the point?

The point is that when this level of new-found success presented itself I was viewed as someone who was beginning to take off and I was a proven earner amongst a new wave of people, unbeknownst to myself, were waiting to see if I could pull some of the things off that I had spoken about over the past few years and now the stage was set.

Like most things you are brought into situations that you are prepared to handle, even if you don't know it yet. I was put in a situation where knowledge of my deals piqued the interest of a good friend and mentor of mine we will call, "Prince". Prince and I were meeting as we always had. We would speak almost weekly for one deal or another.

HTH Designs LLC
2004

I met Prince in 2004. At the time I started a t-shirt company. By chance, we ended up meeting and working together. He taught me about sales, the clothing industry, and business in general. At that point, he had been a businessman for about 15 years and had a wealth of knowledge. He even allowed me the opportunity to work for him. After about a week he fired me.

He hates this story, but it is something that I will never forget; one because I've never been fired from a job and two for the reason he fired me. He wanted me to F.E.A.R my approach.

At the time, I began to learn so much about business and the particular industry. As a seasoned businessman, he saw something in me that I didn't truly understand at the time. He told me I should go into sales. He said I had a gift.

I decided that in order to learn as fast as possible I would volunteer to work for him. In fact, I offered to volunteer and work as an apprentice. Prince wouldn't hear of it. He said he always paid someone for a job.

Perhaps I was better at selling than I knew because I was able to convince him to let me learn the game from the other side. The way I saw it, the more I knew about the process the better the salesman I could become. So, I began to learn the business.

To date I still use the knowledge I gained from that one-week internship. It benefits my clients who I help to grow their new businesses, friends who need referrals for clothing designs, and connections to people who still work in that business.

If things were so good then why would he fire you, Hussain? His answer (and by the way, he hates when I tell this story) was I had too much talent to spend my time doing a laborers job. In fact, throughout my career in education, he told me I was wasting my time as a public-school educator. He saw my intuition and savvy as a businessman, and he pushed me to pursue business.

The way Prince saw it, it's all about providing for your family and leaving the world better than you found it. Why would I work for a fixed salary when I could make 10 or 100 times more a year as a businessman? He was right. F.E.A.R set in and I began to see how with more money and more freedom I could have more joy and I could impact more people.

As a classroom teacher, I could help 30 students a year. As a specialist or even a principal, I could help hundreds or possibly a couple of thousand a year and that would be the ideal. That would assume I agreed with the current political structures surrounding education.

It would also mean I had freedom within my school to facilitate instruction the way I saw fit. During the accountability years in NYC, that wasn't the case.

Teachers spent almost the same amount of time proving their efforts as they spent actually teaching.

I am more of "the spirit of the law" type of guy as opposed to the letter of the law. I live in the gray. Working as a union employee my ceiling was set and my life would be dictated for as long as I subscribed to the prescription that was paid out for myself and others who sought the profession. I opted to pave my own course along with Prince.

Prince had an idea. He saw that I was able to make some larger deals now that I had a new luxury vehicle and on a given day I could wear somewhere in the neighborhood of $75,000 in jewelry. The only thing was that the numbers he was speaking about were way out of my league. I learned a lot about a lot during that conversation.

For the first time I was actually embarrassed by how I presented myself. I learned that it was more important to live the part than to look the part. To look at Prince you'd never know he lived such a comfortable lifestyle. For all the years I've known him I've never seen him in more than $200 worth of clothing including his shoes.

Prince doesn't value labels. He knew so much about how clothes were made and the "behind the scenes" that it was insignificant to him. Think about this, have you ever wondered why most jewelers don't wear an abundance of jewelry? Have you ever noticed that stockbrokers don't own stock?

One more, have you ever been to a car dealership and noticed that the car the dealer is driving isn't one that he or she is trying to sell you? It's because they know the true value of the products and items they are selling you. They understand the markup.

Prince would rather spend time with his family, take vacations, send his children to good schools, and make sure his lineage was set up in case he wasn't around to provide for them. He helped to show me the value of these things in a way that I couldn't see at the time. He also allowed me to F.E.A.R our next business deal.

When I declined Prince's offer to partner on a new deal because I didn't have the capital to invest he made me a deal I couldn't refuse. He gave me the opportunity to become a partner on the venture and told me not to worry about the money; we could figure it out later. I was taken aback. He offered me the chance to get into a deal just because. From that day on, we have partnered on numerous deals and we share 50/50 partnerships on several different business ventures.

I've never asked him why he offered me the prospect of a partnership. My suspicion is he saw the potential of a partnership and I know for a fact that he has full faith and trust in my ability and business ethics. We have spoken about these topics at length over the years.

He also benefited from the proposal I offered Agita. I offered him the package deal just because. I wanted someone to benefit from it. In turn, he made me a partner where Agita scoffed at the notion of giving me a percentage of the profits.

Today I make sure to give back whether it's time, donations, advice, or mentorship. It's my duty to ensure the next wave of young entrepreneurs and school students have exposure to an alternate perspective on how they can achieve their goals, hopes, and dreams. I learned that I didn't have to stop teaching but I did have to leave the institution that confined me. I still work with schools as a volunteer and as a consultant.

The win-win is I still get to work with teachers, students, and business people. The added bonus is I do it on my terms. If you are tired of the shackles set in place to keep you from reaching your maximum potential, remember to F.E.A.R your current approach to your life. Live your life Presidential.

3

LUCK

"If it wasn't for bad luck I wouldn't have any luck at all."
Albert King

2006 Custom Scion TC

2008

Have you ever met or been around someone who seemingly just can't catch a break? No matter the time of day,
the season, or the weather this person always has the
worst "luck"?

My assumption is you have a crystal-clear image of
someone who fits this bill perfectly and at this very
moment you're thinking of some terrible circumstance

they endured. Take a moment. Relive that memory. It sticks out to you for a reason.

Perhaps you have a feeling attached to that person. Perhaps you have a feeling about the very story in your mind and it is that instant that has helped you to determine how you see that individual. I know I do. I have a person, a place, and a thing in my mind that is cemented in my memory. The thought of this person instantly drives me to the idea of, if "oh me, oh my" was a human being.

I have several stories in mind about this person and a slew of tales to tell that reinforce the concept of bad luck. Before I delve into this rabbit hole I would like to remind you Seneca stated, "Luck is where opportunity meets preparation." What his statement means is you create your own luck.

Your actions or inactions determine your odds in accomplishing a goal or achieving failure. Both are pursuits. Generally speaking if you are overweight, broke, underachieving in life it is because of choices you have made over time to place yourself in the exact spot you disdain. If you disagree you might be similar to the inspiration for this chapter.

I know a man who for the purpose of this piece will be called "Bug". Bug is intelligent, handsome, charming, and charismatic. He was raised in a loving household and comes from a good family. He grew up in a house and had two hardworking parents. I know what you're thinking, is this the wrong story? This guy sounds like a dream.

With all the chips seemingly stacked in his favor, you would think this narrative concludes with bright lights and celebrations. You couldn't be further from the truth. And he couldn't be further from success if he tried.

Earl Nightingale defined success as, "the progressive realization of a worthy goal or ideal". Nightingale alluded to the idea that success is a journey and not a destination. In order to be successful, you have to have a goal and the pursuit of that goal is the path of success.

The gentleman I am speaking about has no such passion to date. He does have one pursuit. He is a barber. A long-honored tradition, a respected profession, and art. Again, most of you are perplexed.

You might be asking, why am I saying this good looking, bright, professional doesn't have good luck? It reads as if he has nothing but good luck. Indeed, it seems that way; however, luck, like beauty, is in the eye of the beholder.

From the outside looking in, we could perceive the man in question as a celebrity of sorts, someone to aspire to be like. From interactions with him over the years I can tell you as a matter of fact this is not the case.

· · ·

IN AN EFFORT TO prove my statement I'll share a story that takes place in the mid-2000s. As fate would have it Bug came into an opportunity most workers dream of. He was presented with the chance to go from worker to owner!

After working in a handful of different barbershops over 20 years at that point a family member had a close friend who came into a seven-figure settlement from a lawsuit. This lawsuit recipient was in his early twenties and looked up to Bug. He trusted that Bug had the knowledge and expertise to run his own barbershop and the added bonus: he could be trusted.

His best friend was related to Bug. This young man had the right idea. He came into a lump sum of money and his idea was to invest a piece of it into a business with a businessman who had a client base in an industry that would always have clients. It was a no brainer. What could go wrong?

Well, let's see. Bug took the money and found a store front. He had a catchy name for the shop and he was on a corner in Flatbush, Brooklyn. This was a goldmine. Most businesses can't open because of the startup costs. Bug had that problem solved; he had all the funds required to secure the storefront and to build out the business.

When the time came to set up the shop Bug reached out to family and friends for assistance. From Bug's account, no one wanted any part in building his dream. I remember the first and last conversation we had at the shop. Bug went on to call those he sought aid from "haters". He exclaimed, "Watch when the shop is popping I'm not giving out free cuts, nobody better ask me for a thing".

I felt bad. I felt guilty. Then I remembered, Bug hadn't asked me for help. I also remembered the one and only time Bug was allowed in my car. In the summer of 2006, I financed my first vehicle.

It was a Scion TC. I fell in love with that car the first time I saw it on television in 2004. I knew I wanted it from day one. It was my batmobile. I finally got the chance to get my hands on it and I pounced on the opportunity. I had big dreams for this car. It was my poor man's version of a Lamborghini.

At the time there were aftermarket vertical door kits that allowed the doors to rotate up instead of opening out like a standard door. The sole purpose of purchasing this vehicle was to get those custom doors on my car (against the wise words of my elders including my mother, and longtime friend and mentor "Prints").

I couldn't wait to get my car ready for the summer. I purchased the car in early July just in time for the 4th of July weekend. I made an appointment to have my doors done the day after I drove it off the lot. I had to wait about a week to get the funds to have the car altered so I drove around Brooklyn feeling like a million bucks just waiting for what the rest of the summer had to offer.

While driving around I passed by the barbershop where Bug worked. It was a local shop where I used to attend grammar and middle school so I frequented the neighborhood often. I was headed to my next destination and Bug asked if I could take him home. It was only a few blocks away on a block I grew up on so it was a win-win.

"No problem Bug, get in."

CRUNCH!!

"Yo, what was that?", I asked in anticipation as I peered out of the passenger side view mirror.

Bug replied, "Nothing man, you good."

I was far from good, I was pissed!! There was a huge dent, dead center of my passenger door. The focal point of my new vehicle. A dent that was there because he carelessly (in my mind intentionally) opened my brand new black sand pearl door into a parking meter that was easily two feet away from the car. I parked a foot away from the curb because I didn't want to scratch my rims.There was no excuse to come close to the meter.

I had waited until I owned a rental property that netted enough money to cover the cost of my car note to purchase this car. I'd sacrificed my privacy and lived at home to set myself up for the future with an investment before making a luxury purchase that was now ruined.

Is it obvious I'm getting excited even recounting this event?

When I pointed it out to him he didn't even apologize. No, he looked at it and said, "Damn that's crazy". I should have kicked him out of the car. Somehow, I didn't. I dropped him off. I got out and let him out of the car. He had the nerve to have an attitude and sucked his teeth as if I were exaggerating about the dent that I ended up paying $100 to have removed (thanks Prints for the referral).

What you're not understanding is this car had a fold, if you will, in the door. If the door had been hit anywhere else, more than likely there wouldn't have been more than a nick in the paint at best.

This dent caused a crease in the door that warped the car door and ended up being the size of a sheet of paper because of how it was contorted. I had already paid $1,200 for the deposit on my Lamborghini door hinges. The car was due at the shop within a day or so.

Fast forward a few months back to our conversation at his barbershop. Even after the car door incident (which if you've ever had a dent taken out you know it's not perfect, you can always see a small marker of where the occurrence took place. I know, I know back to the point). Bug was telling me about all of the items he had lined up to get attention for the shop including business cards. I knew I could offer guidance so I decided I should try to lend a hand.

At the time I had a graphic design and printing company called HTH Designs. I could appreciate how he felt as I felt under-supported by those I felt were friends and family at that point.

Bug shared he was going to get a standard set of 1000 business cards for about $150. We are talking about a one-sided white card with a one-color generic simple inlay. At the time I could offer him 1000 double-sided fully custom, full color cards for $75. In addition, I was going to drop them off to him once they were done.

What came next was F.E.A.R. I had a revelation. I offered my services and what he said is tattooed on my brain. He said and this is verbatim, "Why would I pay you when I could pay someone else?"

Cue the fireworks. I almost exploded. Instead, I Forgot Everything And Reset. I removed my ego from the equation. I removed business from the equation. I removed our relationship from the equation. And, at that moment, I removed Bug from my circle.

I learned something about Bug that day and that lesson hasn't escaped me since. Bug had all the opportunities required to be successful yet he was alone when he started his business. Was he alone because he was a habitual dent maker? Was he alone because he didn't reach out to all of his family and friends? Remember he didn't ask for my assistance.

Perhaps he was alone because he deserved to be alone. He didn't do anything to deserve the money he was gifted. He fell into it. Perhaps he didn't appreciate the opportunity. Perhaps if he had a business plan or he struggled through efforts to secure these funds he would have had the wisdom to capitalize on this blessing.

He didn't. Bug's weapon of choice was self-pity. He blamed the world for his blunders. He was unapologetic and ungrateful. He blamed others where the fault was clearly his own. He made the mistake of believing someone owed him something when in reality nobody owes you or Bug anything.

You control your destiny. You control your narrative and you control your mindset. If you look back I mentioned I related to his pain as a new business owner. I did not let the fact that not everyone was going to support my venture stop me. The reasons didn't matter. Focusing on the negative was wasted energy.

To date, Bug is still unsuccessful. His greatest gift is his lack of success as it is a beacon to all those who pursue greatness. His story should serve as a lesson to all who can see that blaming others and not taking account-ability will always land you in the same place. Now with over 30 years of barbershop experience, Bug still rents a chair and has to bounce from shop to shop because he cannot maintain enough clientele to pay his booth rent.

If you find that you are not where you want to be in any aspect of your life, F.E.A.R it. If you don't like your physique, get up and exercise, begin to change your diet.

Change your circle. Do something different. Give yourself a chance. Do not set unrealistic goals and look for an easy way out. You didn't become overweight overnight and you won't get a beach body overnight either. Don't get down on yourself.

Yesterday is gone. F.E.A.R. Today is yours, no more excuses, no more empty wishes, and bad luck. You create your luck. You create your success and your happiness.

4
_____

DIGNITY

Amber Rose: "What do you call a woman who sleeps with a lot of men?"

Jesse Lee Peterson: "A slut."

Amber Rose: "What do you call a man who sleeps with a lot of women?"

Jesse Lee Peterson: "A slut maker."

High School Business Card
1999

Do you believe in double standards when it comes to men, women, and casual sex? If you let popular culture dictate the narrative it might be impossible to see anything but a double standard, especially if you flashback to the '80s and '90s when I grew up.

Think back to any action movie or popular television show. The attractive male always got the girl; it was almost like a reward. Could you imagine James Bond being Jane Bond? How popular would that franchise have been with a female lead who slept with several different men during each movie?

Imagine how differently we might view a popular '90s television show like *Saved By The Bell* if Zack Morris weren't the aggressor chasing his true love Kelly Kapowski, played by Tiffany Amber Theissen.

In most episodes of the show, Zack dated other girls. It wasn't until the addition of A.C. Slater, another attractive ladies' man that sought the attention of Kelly, did the show really focus on the relationship tensions between Zack and Kelly.

On the show, Kelly dated and Zack dated. The volume and pursuits were different. Zack would engage the girls on the show and Kelly was pursued. Kelly was the pretty, sweet, and popular head cheerleader at Bayside High School, what guy wouldn't want to be with her? Now let us assume a role reversal, would we accept Tiffany Amber Theissen's character if she were constantly chasing Zack?

This show always reminded us that the popular guy got the girl. On the same show, Screech, a nerdy, clumsy, and unpopular student, played by Dustin Diamond, chased his true love, Lisa Turtle.

Screech never got the girl, well there were a couple of episodes where Lisa treated Screech with dignity, but they never ended up together. Why would they? Screech was a nerd, a "loser".

What attractive and popular woman would want a smart man who only had eyes for her? The only time Screech found a lasting relationship on the show was when the show's producer, Aaron Spelling, decided to cast his daughter Tori Spelling on the show as Screech's nerdy counterpart, Violet. Perhaps this was just an outlier.

Let us examine another popular show from the '90s, *The Fresh Prince of Bel-Air*. Will Smith's lead role on the show was a young, charismatic, athletic, handsome, and popular ladies' man. He wore nice clothes and was a charmer. Almost every show he dated a different girl and it was acceptable. He pursued "honey's" every week and we loved him for it.

The main character, Will, also had a female cousin named Hilary who was about the same age and dated a lot of men. The interesting distinction between the two was that Hilary was sought after or she only showed interest in men that had power or money. She was also painted as unintelligent and shallow.

The show also had another male co-star Alfonso Ribeiro, who played Carlton Banks, Will's pampered, ambitious (yet again), nerdy cousin. Carlton was constantly in pursuit of a young lady on the show. As always, they threw him a bone when it was comically appropriate.

There was an episode where Will's best friend Jazz, played by DJ Jazzy Jeff had a sister played by Vivica Fox who was attractive and ambitious. She was a catch but as the show progressed she ended up being controlling and seemingly crazy. Will ended up being put in his place of sorts.

This young woman was untamable until Carlton stepped in. The plot twist only worked on the show because Carlton was the least likely candidate to know how to "handle a woman".

Another popular family sitcom was the Chicago based, *Family Matters*. As always there were several teen roles on the show. The teenage male lead was Eddie Winslow, similar to Will on *The Fresh Prince of Bel-Air,* and he had an unintelligent friend who was usually the laughing point of the show. Eddie got all the girls and the world turned.

On the show, Eddie had two sisters. We will focus on the one that was also a teenager, Laura. Laura would eventually become the center of the show once the introduction of her male counterpart, America's favorite nerd Steve Urkel was introduced.

For those who know the show you might remember Steve Urkel was not an original cast member. He was introduced as just another on-off cameo character except his show tested highly and the writers decided to bring him back. His character was so popular the show was written around his character instead of the Winslow family.

Steve pursued Laura each and every episode only to be shot down in comedic and sometimes heartbreaking fashion. It wasn't until the cookie-cutter nerd genius had a Dr. Jekyll and Mr. Hyde-like transformation in his science lab that Steve Urkel became Stefan Urquelle that Laura showed any interest. The actor, Jalil White, played both roles. Except, with the deduction of glasses and other wardrobe changes Steve becoming his alter ego, Stefan, made it acceptable for Laura to date him.

Are you noticing a trend here? If a man is smart, sweet, and shows interest in one woman, he is considered unattractive by attractive women. He has to be dashing, charismatic, and handsome to find affection from an attractive woman. An attractive woman however is to be desired just because.

Hilary Banks wasn't anything outside of pretty. She wasn't a nice person or anything else. The same with Lisa Turtle on *Saved By The Bell*. They cared about their looks and their social standing yet because they were good-looking we looked past their flawed personalities.

Comedian Dave Chappelle has a bit about this phenomenon. He said, "A women's test in life is material. A man's test in life is a woman. Now by test I mean those are the things we desire." He goes on to show the parallels of our daily drives and jokes about men being hunters and why men have nice cars...because women like nice cars and so on.

Growing up these are the images and views I was taught by the most popular and effective method of brainwashing at the time: the television. That coupled with hip hop and my surroundings it was obvious that my pursuit of girls and women growing up was inevitable. In another chapter, we will discuss love at first sight at the tender age of six (6).

This is not an indictment on hip hop culture and rap music. That is to say that we cannot deny the glorification of polygamy and the exploitation of women in the music however let's not act like that doesn't exist with other cultures. I would also like to add that although these themes do exist within the culture these ideals aren't the only layer that is found within the culture. There are many layers to hip hop and its evolution.

Throughout my teenage years, I fit the mold of a typical teenage male. I was even called the black Zack Morris in high school. As a teenager, it was all about fun even though I knew I hurt some feelings and broke some hearts. For that, I do apologize.

As a girl dad (a father of daughters), I couldn't imagine my little ladies being with a young man such as myself at the time. The joke is for guys like us having daughters is karma.

I wouldn't say I was a bad seed or anything too crazy; however, I did like to hang out with girls and I fit the bill of a popular teenager. My idols were only a few years older than I was; this is what they were doing. None of us had dads in our lives and the fathers we did have were womanizers, thus the cycle continued.

I can only think of a handful of people I knew growing up who had dads at home. The dads we knew who were at home also had children with other women during their current relationships; cheating was definitely something the couples had to overcome.

Where I come from, the figures we all wanted to be like were drug dealers, ballplayers, or pimps. It sounds bad from the onset but if you peel back the layers the common thread is we just wanted out of poverty.

I'm sure if we really tried, we could find other similarities between the three different subjects; however, the other two easily identifiable features besides the money are they all have women around them and they are all perceived as liked, respected, or popular within the community. I'd like to remind you that this is the stance of a teenage boy who had only been on one round trip flight ever before the age of 18.

The second time I would take a flight was where the F.E.A.R set in. It was the summer of 2000 and it was time for my high school graduation. I was 18 and ready for what the world had to offer. I didn't apply to colleges because I didn't like school although I graduated with an 88 average. I could have attended an institution of higher education but I knew school wasn't for me and so did my mother.

My mother was an educator at the time and she knew how I felt about my post-high school pursuits and she wanted more for me so she conspired (lol). She and my oldest cousin on her side of the family decided that they were going to get me out of Brooklyn so I wouldn't get into any trouble. My mom and cousin both decided that I should move to Minneapolis, Minnesota.

They made this decision without my knowledge of course and to this day I thank both of them for their lying and scheming (lol). My mom really had to pull the trigger on the deal when I got into a fistfight in my building the day before my high school graduation.

At the time I told her these kids tried to rob me in the hallway. In the building I grew up in, that was extremely possible. The reality was I had a fight with a kid from 3rd Street in my neighborhood. These kids were in a gang. They all sold drugs for a guy who (Rest in Peace) was killed by the co-founder of the gang over a dispute about a year later. He was only in his twenties.

This fight was one of several that took place in the neighborhood over literally nothing. I don't even remember why the fight happened outside of the fact that this kid was my age and he had a problem with one of my friends who was two years younger than me. His fight became mine and other fights took place the same way, where one of my older friends fought someone their age. We all looked out for one another as friends.

Within two (2) weeks I was on a flight to Minneapolis; I flew out literally 20 years ago to this date (wow). My mom told me the flight was a graduation gift. I earned a vacation for my hard work. I couldn't wait. What I didn't know at the time was I only had one ticket; I'd never been anywhere.

I had no idea my mom had no intended return date scheduled. I remember that day like it was yesterday. I remember my farewell tour. All of my friends were at Lincoln High School pool. I went in and said goodbye before heading to the airport.

Moving Day

2000

Minneapolis was an eye-opener in so many ways. We will get into that more later on. For now, let's focus on how a kid from Brooklyn received a warm welcome from women young and old from the first full day I spent in the city. My cousin told me how to get downtown Minneapolis and he wanted me to meet him at his job when he got off so we could come home together.

I spent a few hours downtown by myself; I got lost in the city. I went to different stores and buildings, ate lunch, and made some new friends. At that point, I felt like Will Smith. Minneapolis wasn't Bel-Air but for a kid from Brooklyn, it sure felt like it.

A few months would pass and I ended up staying in Minneapolis. I got the first job I applied to three days after being there as a front desk clerk for a large hotel chain. I met celebrities and all sorts of people at that job. I made new friends and came across some interesting people. One of those people changed my life.

He was someone I looked up to and respected as an 18-year-old. He was a mutual acquaintance. He was just someone who was around. He used to sell my friends weed. I never smoked weed or cigarettes and to this date I still don't but that's what was going on at the time.

We were cool. I used to cut his son's hair. He was my senior by about 15 years. We're going to call this gentleman "Red". Red was an ex-pimp from Detroit. Perhaps if you let Red tell it, to this day he is still pimpin' because pimpin' is a mindset and a lifestyle.

During this time popular songs on the radio were Jay-Z's, "Big Pimpin'", 50 Cent's "P.I.M.P", and other tracks glorifying the vocation. Before, during, and after our interactions, I never thought that being a literal pimp was a cool thing or something worth pursuing.

·   ·   ·

I REMEMBER WATCHING the 1998 HBO special, *Pimps Up, Hoes Down*, and feeling terrible for the women that were living that lifestyle. Like most things perceived from the eyes of an innocent adolescent. As a youth, the portrayals we were allowed to access are glorified caricatures of those who really live these harsh lifestyles.

Something like a "bitch slap" is made fun of and used in jest. As a youngster, unless you saw those things really taking place you would understand that using that term wasn't a joke at all. To bounce back quickly my neighborhood had a stroll. If you're from Brooklyn you know Ocean View Avenue and what it was famous for from midnight until sunrise.

We used to be on the corner so much we knew the ladies who started and ended their shifts on our block in the alleyways. I have seen young girls that we knew get into that life and it was heartbreaking even as a teen.

Back in Minnesota, I remember one-night Red was drunk. I don't drink and I never did which in this instance was probably for the best. I remember getting to the point where I wanted to fight him but the mutual people in the room kept things from boiling over.

This one particular night for whatever reason he was angry. I don't know what got into him or rather how long these feelings were within him but he let loose. He went in on me and on my lifestyle at the time.

"You ain't shit. You think you doing something? These bitches would eat you up out in the game. You ain't no pimp, nigga you's a trick."

Now if you don't know what a trick is, that is not a compliment. A trick is someone who pays for sex, a customer. He continued. This drunken rant literally came out of nowhere.

He came in swinging like Cuba Gooding Jr., in the movie *Boyz N The Hood*. Everyone in the room was quiet just seeing where this speech was going. In the room, I was being coached to stay calm because Red was drunk. He was on truth serum.

At first, I was offended but by the time he was done F.E.A.R had set in. Red basically tried to speak to me as a father figure in the worst way possible. However, his rant was more about my views on myself, my self-worth, and self-esteem. He was saying that by going out with multiple girls at the same time and glorifying how I sought them out that I was missing the point that I was the real prize.

He went on to explain (with a lot more vulgarity and profanity) that I shouldn't be paying for dates or spending money on clothes or jewelry to attract women. He said it should be the other way around and that women should rain over me because I was special.

He explained how these girls who weren't truly worth my time could say that we had been together and that lowered my stock. It was a fresh perspective. My whole life I had sought to chase women to pad my stats and in the interim, I was setting a poor example for those who looked up to me. Imagine how twisted and dysfunctional the culture has to be for a bonafide pimp to have to be the one who explains to a young man he doesn't need a woman to define his worth.

As young men we were lost. We lived a locker room lifestyle in high school, *"As Seen On TV!"*. If you were cool you were supposed to be around girls; it was one of the things that made you cool. The guy who got all the girls, the ladies' man. Now it seems so different.

Red was showing love. He was trying to get me to see that I was wasting my time focusing on girls. I should have been focusing on myself and my pursuits. He might not have said it as eloquently or even at all for that matter.

The point is, that is what I took from the conversation. Red told me he had love for me that night. He said he saw me as a nephew or a son. He was a good father to his child Red the 3rd. He always wanted his son around me because I was a good role model for him. I played sports, I went to work, I was smart and ambitious. Red saw something in me and I'm glad he helped to bring it out.

Sometimes loved ones want to help, they just go about it in a way that isn't conducive to your temperament. As a parent, I learn that lesson often while trying to relay key points, just as Red and others did with me along the way. Within reason, if you can F.E.A.R within the situation you might find a hidden gem, the needle in the haystack.

As a people, we ought to make cool look different. Perhaps Carlton, Urkel, and Screech should be our protagonists. They had good hearts, brains, and ambition. Maybe we should shy away from lifting up the Will Smiths and Zack Morris's at least on popular programming.

Look at what we glorify today. I won't name names, but the people who just popped into your head probably popped into mine too. We have to do better.

5

HUBRIS

"The same honor waits for the coward and the brave.
They both go down to Death."
Achilles in *The Iliad*

My first investment property

2005

Excessive pride is as toxic as alcohol and a woman's scorn wrapped in one. When your best judgment is clouded by nothing but the idea of being correct, you are doomed to a life of massive failures. In this chapter, I will outline a story where logic took a backseat to hubris much like it has since the beginning of time. In this instance, the coward and the brave were both one and the same.

I was once told by a great mentor of mine, "A", that in relationships, "How you start, is how you finish". My understanding of that quote is people rarely change, but circumstances and attitudes change all the time. For instance, in a relationship between boyfriend and girlfriend, a woman might not enjoy a man leaving his work clothes in a pile on the floor in the bedroom after work.

This habit isn't something that seems like such an egregious act; there are certainly worse offenses that take place in a relationship. Over time, three things can happen. The man changes his behavior, the woman changes her opinion on the behavior, or there is turmoil because the problem still exists.

Some might say, well if the man really wanted to be with the woman he should change. Others might say if the woman really wanted to be with the man she should accept him for who he is. A third group might believe they should come to some common ground as successful relationships are about communication and compromises.

The beauty of life is all of these opinions and stances are correct and reasonable. We as humans can disagree on an issue and both be sound in logic. The disconnects in relationships arise when one side believes there is only one way to solve a problem, and any variation or deviation from that stance is incorrect. That belief stems from pride. Pride can be a healthy feeling that brings joy. Much like anything else in life, excess pride can bring you pain and misery.

The lesson learned in the next story began over 30 years ago with a man and a 4-year-old boy. The relationship was one of minimal interactions out of circumstance. The young boy saw the older man as a friend to his mother and the man saw the boy as the son of a woman he was courting. Time passes, gifts are exchanged, dinners are held, and the cycle repeats. Birthday, Christmas, birthday, Christmas, and so on and so on.

This relationship grew over time and we forward 15 years or so. The man we shall call "Agita". It is the late 1990s and Agita has a dear aunt who dies of a degenerative brain disease common amongst the elderly. His aunt loved her nephew and as it would happen, named him in her will. She left Agita a handsome inheritance that he saw fit to invest. One of his investments happened to be real estate.

At the time real estate in Brooklyn, New York was accessible. Properties were relatively expensive compared to other parts of the country or the globe but they were not as high priced as they are now since the recent gentrification of the best of the five boroughs (because we all know Brooklyn is the top of the food chain, ask Mike Tyson).

Agita decided to take his chances on a condominium in a nice neighborhood called Park Slope, named for its best most alluring trait, its proximity to the famed Prospect Park. For those who aren't familiar with the term or concept of a condominium, it is the same concept as a townhome. A condo (for short) is a unit in a community that shares property taxes and management to run the collective group of homes.

Agita did well. His first investment was a condo that cost $140,000. This purchase at its peak swelled to about $600,000 during mid-2010. A sound investment and wealth builder. That area of Prospect Park now known as Windsor Terrace has changed significantly from the time of the purchase to this current point in time.

With his first successful rental investment Agita set his sights on bigger and better. He invested in another larger multi-family property in Brooklyn a few years after his initial purchase.

During this time, I had graduated from high school and was living in the Midwest. I was working for a Fortune 500 company making a considerable amount of money especially considering I was 19 years old and the cost of living was significantly lower than what I would pay in the Big Apple.

My bank account grew and so did my understanding of real estate and the benefits of investing. With my new-found success in the workforce, new-found interest in real estate, and my long-standing history with Agita, it only seemed natural that we partner. Agita didn't seem to have the same sentiment.

Over the next few years, I would beg and plead. I would ask, ask, and ask again for an opportunity to show that I could be a solid investor and partner if just given the chance to get in the game. It didn't quite work out that way. What happened was spite. Yeah, good old, "I know better than you and I can't wait to prove it" spite. That train is never late for one who is filled with pride.

The year is now 2005, I have relocated back to Brooklyn. I work for the city of New York. I am a college student with far less income and savings than I did in 2001 and 2002 because I decided to pursue a more fulfilling career in education. It was very humbling to be back in my mother's house. It was a choice I made for several reasons.

Even in my youth, I believed I could find success anywhere. I wasn't worried about walking away from what was considered and still is considered a great job. I have always believed in myself (my mom did as well). I felt like I should take a shot at purchasing my own place. I didn't want to pay rent.

At the time I believed paying rent wasn't the best use of my funds. The literature I was studying at the time led me to believe ownership was the key.

Agita decided to prove to me that I was in over my head so he issued a challenge. He told me that if I could find an apartment that I liked under $100,000 he would help with the deposit (about $10,000). To this day help was not clearly defined. Rest assured it was not going to be a gift.

A stimulus package for sure but even now, knowing what I know about loans and mortgages I would have been in serious debt as I would have been in a situation where I was taking a 100% loan from two debtors but I digress.

The challenge was set and I was optimistic about what I would find, and what I ended up finding were 350 to 495 square foot studio apartments in neighborhoods that I really didn't want to move to. Agita was right. He knew the market. I had numbers in my head based on what I was exposed to in the Midwest.

At that time $100,000 in the city I lived in I could have purchased a fully detached 3-bedroom 2-bathroom house in a suburb just outside of the city limits. What Agita didn't anticipate was my understanding of investing and my level of dedication to my pursuit of financial independence.

. . .

DURING OUR SEARCH, we did find some gems that made sense to purchase as landlords. I did my research and I found several properties that fit Agita's guidelines.

We found one property that had a special feature that made it the opportunity of a lifetime as a young investor. This studio apartment was a co-op (short for cooperative). A co-op is similar to a condo as the owners share responsibilities for the land and groundskeeping.

The difference is a condo is considered real property so each owner pays their own property taxes. A co-op however is considered stock in a corporation and your stake in ownership is a share equal to your purchase of said corporation.

You have more restrictions in a co-op. For example, if you wanted to rent out your unit, you would have to own for two years and you would have to get board approval to do so or you could face hefty penalties.

This is a common practice amongst co-ops as the board members are usually other shareholders and occupants of apartments in the complexes. You have to apply and get approval from the board to even purchase a unit. The board wants to be able to control who lives amongst them. The concept makes perfect sense; they want to protect their investments and quality of life.

This co-op however had a great opportunity for us. As we found out about the potential investment property, Agita reached out to a friend of his, a local heavy hitting politician who decided he wanted to buy 10 of the units in this complex. With us buying almost a dozen units we were not looked at as a typical investor in this set of buildings.

We were looked at as serious investors. So serious in fact that we were able to take the asking price of $75,000 down to $70,000 and we were able to purchase our unit (not units, the heavy hitter didn't buy in, obviously he knew something we didn't which I would learn later) directly from the sponsor!

Wait, am I the only one who is excited? What you have to understand is the sponsor is the main investor. The sponsor is typically a developer who creates this venture and eventually sells off its stock to make a profit. The sponsor is also above the ruling of the board. No, not clear yet? If we bought from the sponsor, that gave us "sponsor status".

With sponsor status, we didn't have to pay fees, penalties, or get board approval. We were made men, we had diplomatic immunity. We could operate as private owners for a fraction of the price of purchasing a condo.

We win! Well, I thought. Remember that part at the beginning of the chapter? The wisdom I got from Adrian. "How you start is how you finish." Well, I was able to get a glimpse at what would become the turning point and end of my partnership with someone I respected and saw as a mentor at the time.

Agita decided HE was going to purchase the property as he had the cash to do so on his own. I was shocked I can even go as far as to say heartbroken. That was my deal. He wouldn't have even found that apartment if it weren't for me. How could he be so selfish?

I had to do some soul searching. With guidance from my mother, my brother Yusef (Yus), and (for now let's call him) Money E. Banks, another person I respected who owned several properties at that time. I had to F.E.A.R. Money was the most influential voice in my final decision in this specific matter.

He was well respected in the neighborhood for several reasons. If you're from Brooklyn you understand. If you're not, read between the lines, that last sentence was your only hint. His words echoed louder than my mother and my older brother solely because he was unbiased and he was a successful real estate investor. His wisdom came from a business perspective and I had the proposal of choice to seal the deal.

My mom, big bro, and Money all stated the obvious. My emotions were mixed because of the personal relationship I had with Agita. My mom warned both Agita and me about entering any business dealings with one another. Yus pointed out that's who Agita always was, this was just my way of finding out. Money stated his opinion in a much more firm and direct manner.

. . .

IT WAS a cool summer night in Brooklyn. Money, myself, and several others were sitting on my grandmother's stoop in front of the house. It was late, Money had his signature bottle of beer. In almost his exact words he stated, "Hussain, that man ain't yo daddy. He don't owe you shit."

He was right. Money is an older Jamaican man. His voice had a slight twang to it. He went on to ask if I really wanted the property and he also shared another piece of information that stuck with me and F.E.A.R set in.

Money asked me how much I want to be a part of this deal. I told him it meant the world to me. He told me to think about it and make sure Agita let me in. He also told me once I buy it, never sell it. He said use it to buy another property and continue the pattern.

At the time I didn't really have a full understanding of what he meant exactly. I knew that by adding assets, more assets would come because of the laws of compounding. What I didn't know were the leveraging methods I know now and use daily to grow my real estate portfolio.

I took heed to every word that was given and I worked myself into the property. Agita moved forward with the purchase process as he intended. but I was able to find my way in. At the time I only had about $2,500 to spend on a $70,000 purchase. I wasn't anywhere near being a 50% partner with that amount of cash. I had to find a way. At the time I was reading a book called *OPM: Other People's Money*, written by Michael A. Lechter.

In the book, the author explained that you have to find a way to close deals. It also had a chapter on paying your entry fee. An entry fee is a price you have to pay for not being able to make the deal on your own.

An example of an entry fee is interest on a loan. You want something today that you can't afford, that could be a house, a car, a vacation, whatever. The entry fee you pay to have that item or experience today instead of missing out could be 32% interest. It could be more. The concept is not a new one. The application of the concept; however, now that was novel.

I went to Agita with a proposal. I broke it down very simply. The purchase price of the house was $70,000 with $3,800 in closing costs and fees. My share would have been $37,600 and remember I only had $2,500 in the bank.

I decided to overpay for my fair share of the investment. I told Agita that he could keep my share of the profits about $250 a month for up to one year (a $3,000 value) as payments towards my debt. In addition, I would also pay all of the closing costs saving him $1,900 in upfront costs.

· · ·

ALL HE HAD to do was give me a year to pay off my
half. If I didn't I would lose my stake in the property and
the money I invested. It was a win-win-win for him.
How could he refuse? In fact, he didn't. He jumped on
it and signed on the dotted line. I mean it was a solid
line but you get the idea.

What he didn't know was that I had an idea. My
idea was that if he agreed, I was going to use OPM to
fund my side of the deal. I didn't know exactly how
but I knew my first task was to land the deal and I
passed with flying colors. Once I was in the deal, my
next step was filling out credit card applications; four
to be exact. This was a time before smartphones and
apps.

Things moved a lot slower so I was able to attain
four new cards at the same time, all with zero interest
balances for up to 18 months. That, coupled with my
current credit cards, gave me a total of $40,000 in poten-
tial credit. I maxed out all of the cards and paid Agita
within two (2) months. I had all of the money at closing
and I received every penny I was entitled to from day
one.

From that point on, we were partners. As time
passed, there were a few occasions where Agita and I
signed deals for loans where I borrowed money from
him with interest and I always paid him back early. As
the months went by, the property value swelled to

$99,000. I believed we should sell, he wanted to hold and there we met our first impasse.

Our first tenant decided to move and we couldn't commit to the $950 rent we initially started out with. To add to our headaches, the management company changed at the complex and they wanted us to pay penalties and cease renting our unit as it was against building guidelines. The penalty was $1,000 and a monthly nonpayment fee of $35 was added to our monthly invoice. This drove Agita mad. Seeing a debt and fighting with the management company took a toll on him.

He eventually got the total balance adjusted off but he wanted to sell. It was 2008 - 2009 and we were in the midst of one of the worst housing bubbles we had ever experienced as a country. We couldn't sell the unit for $80,000 at this point. My opinion changed and I believed it was worth holding on to because prices would rise again. The management issue didn't bother me because I knew we purchased from a sponsor.

Agita wanted out so I bought him out around 2010. I paid him $40,000 for his share of the property. I eventually ended up renting the unit out for $750. A third management group took over and they decided to charge the original $1,000 fee monthly.

Management did not stop their pressure. The debt rose to $7,000. The worst part is, the unit was all mine,

Agita now no longer invested in the property, and I couldn't find the proof that was required to defend myself against management.

To stop the bleeding, I ended up using the property for business purposes. I had to prove I wasn't renting the unit and I wasn't. Management did random inspections and saw the vacant unit so the billing ceased. It even came off my invoice. But the balance didn't go away. More details on this later.

This turn of events soured me towards Agita but I was still optimistic. At the time I chalked it up to inexperience and a lesson learned. This is what comes when you invest. You win some, you learn some. No big deal.

I eventually sold the unit and during the process I came across another condo that was valued over $100,000. I had an in because my real estate agent knew I was closing on the sale and coming into a lump sum of cash. I was able to purchase a 1-bedroom condominium for $50,000. It was a steal. No bank would finance the purchase because the development was affected by the storm Hurricane Sandy.

I could rent the unit for $1,100 and I would walk away with a nice five figure profit on top of a new investment. Everything was amazing. I offered Agita an opportunity to join in on the purchase, he passed. He thought it was too risky.

· · ·

I CONTINUED to invest and I began investing in Houston, Texas. I sold my condo for $130,000 and purchased two condos that grossed $1,950 in rent. Again, I offered Agita an opportunity to be 50/50 partners on both deals he declined. Too risky. He felt it wasn't safe to invest in because the condos were too far away. Who could blame him?

The year is now 2016. I own 4 rental properties in two cities in Texas. Agita owns one (he sold the multifamily because it was a money pit), the one bedroom in Windsor Terrace. I own a co-op in the highly gentrified area of Downtown Brooklyn called Clinton's Hill. I bring Agita to maximize a deal he was presented and it nets me a $50,000 payday at zero interest.

You have to remember from day one Agita never gave me anything; however, he would lend. I am grateful for the opportunities, I just want to be clear on the terms of this $50,000. I was able to secure a $50,000 loan that I had to pay back at $500 per month.

At this point, I have seen the light and I believe I have proven myself as a real estate investor and a trustworthy businessman. I formed my second LLC. Business is growing.

I have a new partner in one condo; all is well. With this new-found knowledge I have, I come across the best opportunity I have ever been presented with to date. The $50,000 I received was basically spent. Agita spent his $50,000 too. He decided to refinance his loan, and in exchange for a higher interest rate, his loan payment would drop.

I didn't like the terms so I didn't want to change our agreement. He decided that as long as I paid the same rate he would waive the interest. The way he saw it since his payment dropped he would be pocketing an additional $100 even with the lack of interest. I agreed.

During his refinance he also pulled out an additional lump sum. His idea was to spend $100,000 on a condo in Florida that would bring him about $1,300 a month in gross rent. With my new knowledge I told him about an investment opportunity that he could benefit from where he would net $6,000 a month with the same investment!!

Let me play that back. He was happy to gross $1,300 with his $100,000 investment. He would have profited about $400 a month after all was said and done. I had a deal lined up that would have grossed him around $10,000 a month and his take home profit would have been $6,000. Fifteen times more than what he was going to make. He was ecstatic.

Here is where everything fell apart and excessive pride set in. I did not have any money to invest in the venture. At this time, I was not involved in property management, however, I did own a property in the city and I had plans on continuing to invest in the city as the opportunities there were off the charts.

All I did was scout the properties, find the management company, run the numbers, and find a bank to finance the whole deal. I didn't want ownership or a stake in the deal. I knew enough about Agita that it would take a bludgeoning to buy into this deal.

I was also happy to pass along the information. I am glad to see those I care about succeeding. If I can't benefit from a deal, it is a great feeling to be able to pass it along to someone on my team.

THE CONVERSATION WENT something like this:

HA: "I found this great deal; you will net $6,000 a month. I have everything all set up all you have to do is make the calls and start the process."

Agita: "That sounds great. Will you be out there to check on things?"

HA: "Yes, I already invest there and I'm looking to grow in that area and the surrounding areas."

Agita: "It sounds great. I'd like to look into it."

HA: "Awesome, can I ask you for a favor?"

Agita: "Uh Oh. I smell a catch..."

HA: "Hear me out."

Agita: "Go ahead."

HA: "Would you consider letting me out of my $500 monthly payments if this all goes through?"

And that is where the conversation ended and the argument ensured.

SO MANY THINGS were said including:
"You think I'm someone off the street?"
"You think you can fast talk your way to the top?"
"You should be ashamed of yourself."
"I can't believe you're your mother's son."
"I look at you as a son and you treat me like this?"

YUP ALL OF THAT. Now you know how on sitcoms they always have this episode where something happens and throughout the show each character tells their story and it's wildly different from the actual event?

This is exactly how that conversation took place. The quotes are quotes. The details are facts and they can all be proven as a matter of public record in terms of the real estate transactions. The conversations again are statements. Those quotes are burned in my mind.

They are constant reminders and motivation. They were also a cause of F.E.A.R. The argument ended with the following terms that I set:

- We (Agita and I) will never discuss business again. And to this point we have not.
- I will continue to pay my $500 monthly payment interest free and not a penny more.

A couple of days later I got a phone call. It's Agita. As if nothing happened he asked a tax question. He was new to the LLC game and he wanted to know about investing in Florida and the benefits it could have for him. My response, "Dude, we don't speak about business. Call your tax guy."

He honestly thought that I would need him before he needed me. He forgot that business included my expertise on anything that could generate income not us partnering on a joint investment.

At the current time, I still have a balance due of $24,500 or 49 more payments. And as a man of my word the last payment will be made in 49 months not a day sooner than required.

In the two years since our disagreement Agita has since purchased two $100,000 condos in Florida. His investment portfolio includes three rental properties. The first investment made in Windsor Terrace and the two condos in Florida.

On this date in time, May 14th, 2020, I am involved in six renovations taking place concurrently in three cities. My company is involved in multiple closings a

week including (if all goes well with closing dates) our
first million-dollar month.

I am also lining up the opening of a new office in
Philadelphia, Pennsylvania to manage all of the investments I have taken a part of for myself, my partners, and
my clients. Our company operates in multiple states
across the country and we are ever expanding. Did I
forget to mention I shared the opportunity with a
friend? This friend felt so honored to be approached
with such an outstanding deal he offered me a 50/50
share of the venture.

That deal was a major contributing factor to the
growth and successes I am able to enjoy to this date
including early retirement from formal education. Not
bad for a kid who started investing in real estate with
only $2,500.

I used to wonder if my request was too outlandish.
Those thoughts no longer exist. I had to Forget Everything And Reset. Nothing I can do can change that
argument. I came away from that situation with a new
perspective on business.

Emotions have no place in the conference room.
Feelings might arise but not emotions. Feelings come
and go. Emotions are much deeper. Without getting too
far off on that discussion my takeaway from the proposal
was more about the terms of the relationship than the
terms of the deal.

If you have sincere intentions and you mean well for all involved in any situation you should proceed with honesty. If anyone is hurt or offended you should consider your approach as an attempt to grow as a compassionate human being. The reflection however shouldn't end there. You should also assess your relationship with the person who had ill feelings and take inventory of your beginnings.

Have you changed, has the other party changed, or are you both at a breaking point. Growth is natural and relationships end; it's a part of life. If you can take something away from each meaningful interaction then you have won. You have gained something. In this case F.E.A.R is a good thing. You can always adjust if you Forget Everything And Reset.

6

DEVELOPMENT

"You are who you are no matter where you are"
Unknown

Freshman Year

1996

Imagine you woke up this morning and you had a check for a million dollars tax free. What would you do with it?

Common answers include:

Pay off debts

Buy a house

Buy a new car

Buy my mom a house

Go shopping

Take a vacation

Invest

Donate some

Save it

My assumption is you have a few of these on your list in some form or fashion. Some say I'd spend $500,000 on a house, others $250,000 on a home. Some say I'd blow $100,000; others say I'd spend $20,000 on myself. Whatever your answer there really is no "correct" answer.

There are answers that could lead to you being in worse debt than what you started with. There are other choices that will deplete your million quickly and options exist that would help you grow your million into multi millions, and beyond.

In this chapter, I will share a story about someone who basically woke up to that exact scenario. We will call this person "CLK" after the luxury car. CLK went from hundred-aire to millionaire in one shot.

CLK was anticipating this day as she knew the lump sum was going to hit her bank account in advance. She reached out to me and assured me that she wanted to invest her funds. I made sure that she knew my company would be there for her when she was ready.

· · ·

THE TIME CAME and we received a call. CLK called us and like most new investors she was apprehensive about giving away a chunk of money almost as fast as her lump sum was deposited. After some discussion and guidance, she decided that she would spend a relatively small amount. The amount was $40,000 or about 4% of her money. She wanted to dip her toe in the pool before going all in. That idea was smart considering how she accumulated her capital.

Her first idea was to buy a multi-family building that would cost her about five to six hundred thousand dollars. Her only problem was she wanted to stay in Brooklyn, New York. This was a good idea. She wanted to be in a position where her, her children, and her grandchildren could live. She wanted to take care of her family. Unfortunately, that range was not realistic for a duplex in the 718 (that includes Queens, New York).

Her next option was to buy a large home in Atlanta, Georgia. She would spend about $300,000 and let her investments maintain her lifestyle. This option was better than the first, however, we spoke on it and it didn't seem like the best option for her in my opinion. CLK had never owned a home and did not understand (like most non-homeowners) that just because you own your home, your bills don't stop.

On a home with 3,500 square feet you will always have fees including: homeowner's insurance, a home warranty program (if you're a seasoned homeowner), lawn care, pool maintenance, pest control, home security, and property taxes. On a house that size in Georgia, we are easily talking about a set of unforeseen expenses that exceeds $1,000 a month.

This home was also intended to be in a gated community, which meant CLK would have to pay for homeowners association fees or an "HOA". An HOA is a shared cost that covers the maintenance for everything outside of your property that is within the communal space of the community. The management company for the community would be responsible for things like the gates that surround the gated community.

The maintenance, and if there is a security guard, the collective membership fees would pay that salary. The fees would also go to the lawn and gardening expenses on any items on the land, the dues would also be spent on the shared property that is within the gates but not on her specific property like the driveways to her home.

These fees vary depending on the amenities such as if there is a gym, a community pool, a spa, a tennis or basketball court, etc. Her HOA fee in this specific community was a few hundred dollars. Added with the other unforeseen costs, she was in over her head.

· · ·

SHE BELIEVED she could live with $500,000 for at least 10 years assuming a budget of $50,000 per year. She didn't factor in the fifteen to twenty thousand dollars a year that she would have to spend to live in her home that was paid off. CLK (like most overnight millionaires) also forgot one of the biggest expenses when it comes to a new home ownership, FURNISHING.

So many of my clients do not take into consideration the price tag associated with owning a new and larger home. You have beds, couches, tables, electronics, appliances and so on. Coming from a rental in Brooklyn and transitioning to a multi-bathroom, multi-bedroom unit with a backyard and a great room, etc. you might not realize how expensive items are.

The cost of blinds or curtains for a large window are vastly higher than what you would pay for a typical 32 inch by 60-inch set of Venetian blinds that might cost you eight to twenty dollars. We are talking 90 by 120-inch sets of windows in a living room alone. These are items you need a ladder to install. 20-foot ceilings that require a service call or a 14 foot ladder ($200) just to change a light bulb.

These numbers disheartened CLK. My suggestion was to rent the same style home and invest more of her funds to increase her monthly cash flow. That would allow her to be in a situation where she could afford to buy a home this size at some point if she felt the need (although, I believe personal home ownership is a bad investment, details later). She would also have an additional $300,000 to play with even after decorating her home.

Here's the breakdown:

BUYING A HOME (UNFORESEEN EXPENSES):

Home Inspections - before you spend $300,000 on a property you should spend $500 or so to have someone tell you about the roof, foundation, hvac system, electric and plumbing just for starters.

Mortgage Deposit - most people aren't going to buy a home outright especially at the $300,000 mark. To secure a mortgage you're looking at a 10% deposit ($30,000 on a $300,000 purchase) or if you qualify 3% down ($9,000 on a $300,000 purchase).

Closing costs - yes, yes good old closing costs. Surveys, title insurance, bank origination fees, notary and preparation costs, etc. Simply put, the last grabs at your funds before you sign your life away. The closing costs on a $300,000 purchase in Georgia: my rough estimate would be somewhere in the neighborhood of $8,000.

Reserves - Any homeowner can tell you all it takes is

a bad storm and you are out thousands in wind damage that could affect your roof, siding, or structure; even if you are just considering your insurance deductible (and good luck with insurance). Those beautiful trees you have in your front lawn or backyard, they can cost you tens of thousands if the tree roots compromise your sewage line.

TRUE STORY, the first time I saw my first (and last) personal home purchase with my own eyes I was greeted with a $17,000 estimate for this exact issue. I had a home inspection done and all of the plumbing worked just fine. This issue took a few months to really rear its ugly head.

Long story short, it is now almost 3 years later and I am still financing this bill (I ended up spending $12,000 but please note as an investor, I would never spend $12,000 in a lump sum on anything I could finance at 0%).

NOW BANKS KNOW these things happen all too often. To safeguard their investment as your first lien holder they require anywhere from three to six months' worth of mortgage payments in an account they have access to for the first three to six months of your loan.

On a home that costs $300,000 assuming a 10% deposit you would be financing $270,000. Let's also assume a 4% interest rate with a 30-year term. Your monthly mortgage payment would be roughly $2,000 a month including $250 for homeowner's insurance, $460 for property taxes and $1,289 for your principal and interest payments). Your reserves could range from six to twelve thousand dollars.

THAT BRINGS your pre-move in total to:
$30,000 - loan deposit (assuming 10%)
$ 1,000 - home inspection
$ 8,000 - closing costs
$ 6,000 - reserves (assuming 3 months)
$45,000 - pre-move in total.

LET'S assume you decided to rent that beautiful 3,500 square foot home. Let's assume your rent was $3,000 a month. Your move in costs would include:

$ 75 - APPLICATION fee (and that's high)
$3,000 - security deposit
$3,000 - first month's rent
$3,000 - last month's rent (worst case)

$9,075 - total move in costs

WHICH AMOUNT WOULD you rather spend?

Before I could get CLK to lock into a number I had to show her that the best use of her new-found capital was not spending it, but to save money. This concept is one that has kept families from accumulating wealth for generations.

The idea that if I don't have bills I can save money to invest is one of the fastest ways to stay poor. If you are fortunate enough to come into a lump sum DO NOT use that new-found money to pay off bills, or to make new bills (such as a new car, or a new home).

We finally settled on $40,000 as previously mentioned. We settled on this number because at the time of our work together I knew the best bet for her would be a multi-family dwelling. I knew that in the city of Philadelphia, Pennsylvania CLK could purchase a duplex that would net her a return of 20% of her investment and she would have two paying tenants.

I like the idea of a multi-family unit for new investors who can afford to make this type of investment because if you compare this type of purchase to a single-family investment your risk of having to contribute money during a vacancy is certain.

. . .

LET me explain (yay more math):

Single family home - 3 bedroom

Purchase price $60,000 (20% deposit)

$ 1000 - monthly rent

-$ 273 - (loan payment 48k @ 5.5% 30yr loan)

-$ 100 - landlord insurance

-$ 150 - property taxes

$ 523 - monthly bills

$ 523 - potential expense during a vacancy

THE OWNER WOULD HAVE to pay all of the monthly bills out of pocket.

Duplex - 1-bedroom units

Purchase price $60,000

PURCHASE PRICE $60,000 (20% deposit)

$ 1000 - monthly rent ($500 per unit)

-$ 273 - (loan payment 48k @ 5.5% 30yr loan)

-$ 100 - landlord insurance

-$ 150 - property taxes

$ 523 - monthly bills

$ 23 - potential expense during a vacancy

· · ·

IN THIS SCENARIO the landlord would only have to pay $23 out of pocket. The second tenant would pay the first $500 in bills with their rent money.

I worked with (and still do) a private lender that would work with a brand-new investor as long as the investment purchase price was at least $100,000 and the client had a deposit of 20% (a minimum of $20,000). This lender has high closing costs and interest rates including a loan origination fee or two (2) points or (2% of the purchase price), plus, their appraisal fees and other costs. The benefit of working with a company like this is you get the loan.

I am a firm believer in paying my dues. If I am starting a new corporation with no track record of making profits and no documented history showing I can make a profit, why would I expect the best rates? The banks charge more fees and interest because as a new investor or business you are a higher risk. This is the cost associated with starting up.

You have to pay to play. Some people decide not to jump in the game because they feel the cost is too high. For them that's the right decision. For myself and my clients we see the benefits in getting started and refinancing.

CLK had faith and she was comfortable with the amount that she had to invest for the return she expected. She was anticipating about a 35% ROI, therefore, she would see her total investment back in just under 3 years in addition to the benefits of the tax write-offs, the growth in equity she would receive, the property appreciated in value, and the tenants paid down her mortgage. We began to work.

MARCH 2019 - ACCOUNT Balance $850K
Business Account Balance $40K

WE FOUND A PROPERTY FOR CLK; we began her incorporation process and the ball was rolling. Here is where we encountered our first bump in the road. Credit. CLK has advised us that she had been working with a credit repair specialist to boost her scores in preparation for a home purchase. She was using a popular credit app on her smartphone to track her progress.

As some of you know this app and others like it are third party. What that means is they are typically estimated or outdated scores. This app in particular only shows two of the three credit scores and to qualify for the loan required to purchase this property CLK had to have a minimum average score of 640.

Her average score was 619. Two of her scores were above 640: the two that the app showed on her smartphone. This inquiry dropped her scores a few points to pour salt in the wound. This setback was painful for her as it was a shot from out of left field. We encouraged her to stay the course.

The loan company was able to pull her score again during a three-month window of time without affecting her score with another hard inquiry. CLK had plenty of resources to correct the issue as the detrimental items on her credit were a few thousand dollars. She could easily pay these items off, spike her scores and we could close on the deal.

MAY 2019 - Account Balance $720K
    Business Account Balance $38K

A FEW WEEKS had passed and it was time to reassess CLK's scores. She decided to continue to work with her credit repair specialist in lieu of paying off the debts to spike her scores. We knew that the third-party smartphone app wasn't going to give us the most accurate account of information but we still used it as a guide.

Two months had gone by surely something would pop up on this app as she was actively paying her debts and working with someone who was going to handle the troublesome areas of her credit reports. Well, to my surprise the scores dropped.

I couldn't understand how the scores could have dropped if she was working with someone specifically to repair her scores and she was paying off her debts. I had access to her bank accounts as I was the go between for her and the lender. The lender raised a question about the decline in her bank balances. He asked me about her spending habits.

I spoke with CLK and she explained. With new money she had new friends, new family members (who all had problems only her and her money could solve), and she wanted to have a little fun. This was the first time in her life where she could treat herself and her children to some things that she felt they deserved to have. It was just so coincidental that at the very time that she had such good financial fortune those around her had such misfortune with their finances. It's funny how that happens.

CLK had a good heart and a bad accounting system. Her response to being low on cash, go get some more cash. She paid thousands in withdrawal and cash out fees. She also flew first class with her family, bought expensive bags, shoes and accessories for herself, and loved ones. She even gave one of her family members a loan for $25,000.

. . .

THIS WAS one of the toughest decisions for CLK. The reason this one hurt the worse is because this family member was a self-proclaimed woman of God. Her husband is a very well respected and high-ranking member of the church. They are multimillionaires in fact. She thought it was a no brainer to loan her family member this money.

When we spoke about it she did mention one point that would drive a bull mad (that would be a huge red flag). She asked for the money and said please be sure not to mention it to her husband. Now isn't that odd? Why would a married person ask for such a substantial loan and not want their significant other to know about it? This made me sick. The writing was on the wall and it read, "CLK = ATM, all S - O - B stories welcome".

We decided that since her scores weren't going to pick up in time that maybe she should make some smaller cash purchases to start her cash flow streams. We looked into Detroit, Michigan and found the hype was just that, "hype". Now extremely frustrated she wanted to quit the process all together. I assured her all she had to do was be patient.

Finding her great investment opportunities wasn't an issue. Her money was still safe in her account (or was it?); she had nothing but write-offs up to this point. She would see that her scores would increase and this was just a part of the game. We had to do the research.

Sometimes things start off rocky. Sometimes you see a gem, you pay for a home inspection, and you find the gem is a moissanite and not a diamond. Better to spend $500 and walk away, than to commit to $100,000 and be stuck with a money pit. My tolerance and her tolerance differed.

I have developed a thicker skin over the years. She had never done anything like this before. Every dollar going out the door hurt, as it was compounded by (what I would later discover) was a hole in her bank account that could never be sealed.

JUNE 2019 - ACCOUNT Balance $600K
Business Account Balance $38K

THE 90-DAY CREDIT window has now closed. It is time to reapply, and I've noticed it's harder and harder to reach CLK. She had fallen ill. I can only speculate but my belief is the whirlwind of vultures ever hovering above CLK just waiting for another opportunity to pounce, drove her into a dark space. That coupled with frequent vacations and the dwindling finances in her account only exacerbated any other underlying health issues she already had. We had a choice to make and CLK began to crack.

There was a time during our working relationship when I visited CLK to have a face-to-face meeting. She had to pay for an inspection fee so I stopped by to get some face time. Whenever possible I like to meet in person. I find technology insincere and impersonal.

She looked tired. She asked one of the seven or eight people in her apartment at the time to go and grab her purse. Her purse was in the other room and she pulled out a two-inch-thick stack of cash. The money roll was mostly freshly printed $100 bills sprinkled in with some fifties and twenties thrown in the bag.

As she pulled the money out she exclaimed, "Uh uh, I'm missing some money!" I was as shocked as her as the room full of the now dumb, deaf, and blind entourage carried on as if CLK didn't just say that loud enough for all to hear. It was as if it were a common phrase amongst the bunch.

I digress. CLK accused me of stealing from her. She felt that during this whole process all she was doing was paying myself and my partners money. She hadn't seen any results and her time was being wasted. She seemingly forgot the fact that she couldn't qualify for a loan because of her poor credit.

Her "allies" also made sure to tell her that the rates and fees were high and their people could do way better if she would just work with them. At this moment I had to F.E.A.R. This wouldn't be the first time I was accused of such a thing, and I'm sure it won't be the last.

In a world where there are so many scam artists and fine print, I can understand her point of view. I write that based on my perspective today. At that moment, I was infuriated. How dare she or her crew of flunkies fix their faces to ever speak my name in a distasteful manner?

Luckily, I was prepared for this type of situation. I have always had great role models and mentors set in place to give me wisdom in advance. The beauty about wisdom is, you never know when it will become useful.

I was fortunate enough to be a guest speaker at a seminar in Mesa, Arizona just about a year prior to this encounter. One of the other speakers at the event, the keynote in fact, was actress, Desreta Jackson.

During her speech, she spoke about people not being able to see past themselves. She said (and I'm paraphrasing), a liar is always going to see other people as liars because that's who they are. A thief is always going to see others as thieves because that's who they are and so on and so on.

She then went on to explain that's why honest and good people always get taken advantage of. She said it was because they can't see past their good nature. They expect others will do the things they would do and thus they become prey.

At the moment, that concept was novel and ground-breaking to me. As you can see, I never forgot her words or the message. This applied to CLK's situation perfectly.

She was, and possibly still is, in a dark place. She could only see what she was living. Imagine if all day, every day, all you experience is the worst of what the world has to offer; meaning, you are the call everyone makes when they have a problem. They never called to check on you before your million-dollar net worth, but they sure are concerned now. And wait, how did they even get your number?

What CLK forgot was a very important detail. People were calling her, and she reached out to me. She had to call around and get my number. My business luckily (remember we create our own luck) was, and still is, growing with her or without her. She also forgot her loan denial and high rates were due to her being high risk, her low credit scores, and even significantly lower bank balances.

She couldn't take accountability until she was forced to see what she had created. I give her credit; most people aren't prepared to do so. She did. We agreed to take her investment to Texas, where my work as a flipper began to take off, and I guaranteed she would be able to find a deal where she would profit.

. . .

AUGUST 2019 - ACCOUNT Balance $300K
Business Account Balance $39K

WE GAVE Philly one last run. CLK had to commit to a bit more of an investment as prices continued to meet expectations and steadily increase. We found a 2-unit multi-family for about $140,000. CLK had to deposit $10,000 to hold the deal and she began her loan process for the second time officially. Again she was denied due to her credit scores not improving. I was shocked. She blamed the credit repair person. She said she believed they were taking advantage of her and her money.

What I later came to find out was her credit was being repaired. As soon as it was resolved, she would get new store cards at high-end retailers and max her credit limits out. I continued to work with her because I felt maybe someone was taking advantage of her. But now it was time to get back her $10,000.

I made sure she got just that. I spoke with the lender and the seller and organized everything. She was expecting her refund. I knew that was money in the bank but that was the least of our problems.

SEPTEMBER 2019 - ACCOUNT Balance $120K
Business Account Balance $38K

Some time has passed, and my business has continued to grow. I hadn't heard from CLK in a few weeks, and it's time to see where we are with her next steps. CLK and I have a conversation about her credit and what she feels is the best move for her.

Her credit (no longer a surprise) is right where we left it. As time would have it, the prices in Philly increased, and she couldn't find a multi-family unit that would bring her the returns we originally sought.

The loan companies I was working with, and continue to work with, wouldn't finance her because her credit and her business history didn't fit their guidelines. So, I decided to finance her myself. At the time, I was working on a flip that was funded with cash and it was currently in process.

We worked out a deal where CLK would put a $50,000 deposit down on the property, and I would hold the note (become the bank and give her a mortgage). This deal was set up to give her a chance to show her rent rolls and have her first year of taxes done while allowing her the opportunity to repair her credit.

OCTOBER 2019 - ACCOUNT Balance $>50K
Business Account Balance $25K

.   .   .

THE HOMES in Texas are almost done, and it is time to close the deal. It has been a long winding road, chock full of bumps and detours. I am headed back to New York City to finalize the deal with CLK, and I am excited for her. I knew she had a tough year, and this was going to be a new beginning. I tried to contact her several times, and I couldn't reach her. This was odd because she knew I was coming to the city. Out of the blue, I get a call from her sister.

Her sister explains to me that CLK is very upset and embarrassed. I was confused. What could she be so upset and embarrassed about? CLK's sister shared some sad and frustrating news. CLK has spent almost all of her money.

Her accounts were just around $50,000 in total. I was not happy at all. I told CLK's sister that the three of us had to have a three-way call to sort all of these details out. How could she have spent the money that she had saved for this very deal?

Why hadn't I tied up her funds to ensure she couldn't allow this to happen? The answer was obvious. I saw her bank statements, and it became clear as day. She had a problem. I believe, to date, this affliction is one she is still haunted by and I hope she receives some therapy to find a possible root of this disease.

CLK, her sister, and I spoke briefly. The conversation was one where her tone was unapologetic, defensive and disheartening. She was so close. During that call F.E.A.R kicked in and I realized something about CLK, business, and myself. The first feelings and emotions that I felt were anger and frustration followed by commiseration. The realization that CLK didn't purposefully intend to put me in a bad position quickly sunk in.

Immediately the wheels began to turn. When in crisis mode some people tend to focus on the cause of the problem. My (almost) automatic response is solution finding. I had to itemize my next steps and find a way to compensate for a $50,000 lump sum payment I wasn't going to receive. This is a skill I developed over time.

At times people lose hair, lose sleep, develop addictions to controlled substances or they quit. I'm sure there are other options in that spectrum but the typical response to this type of stress is some sort of breakdown either physically or mentally.

For those who don't know this catastrophic event took place just a few weeks after my retirement. This was a significant setback. I welcomed the challenge. Let me be clear, I do not wish for hardship in any form, however, I do understand that hardship is a part of life in particular, the life of a businessman.

"The setback is for the get back." I understand the road of success is like a two-step, you can go from right to left in the blink of an eye. They are remembering you end up right again just as fast.

CLK needed everything yesterday. She had a life changing event happen to her and she wanted to start living the life she always wanted instantly. Unfortunately, for her the lifestyle she wanted cost more than a million dollars cash. Invested wisely she could be in that dream house in Atlanta with new cars and tenants, and investments footing the bill. She lacked patience and discipline. Who could blame her? CLK was like many others who came into lump sums with no education in finance.

Think about it for a second. How much do you have in the bank? How long have you been working? What happens when you get a lump sum (tax return, bonus at work, third check twice a year for those who are not paid monthly)? How much do you own? Before we judge let's reflect on our own actions.

Many of you were drawn to this book looking for answers because you're tired of being on the proverbial hamster wheel. You have to know it starts with F.E.A.R. You have to let go. We all have different things holding us back. Once you realize the power is within you, and only you, to make a change in your life you will see that your opportunities begin to pile up.

Perhaps for CLK this blunder was a greater lesson that money doesn't buy happiness. For the time being, I know one thing for sure. If she is able to bounce back from this experience, it will have to start with Forgetting Everything And Resetting.

She will have to let go of ego, regret, anger, shame, and embarrassment, and focus on what she learned. She will have to take inventory of what worked and what didn't. She will have to own up to her mistakes and find the humility in the situation.

There are so many stories of rags to riches to rags to riches stories out there. Most multimillionaires have a story of a great setback that caused them to catapult into a new realm with their new-found wisdom and resilience. You don't have to blow a million dollars in a year to realize that isn't the best decision to make if your goal is financial freedom, yet if you have wasted a lump sum of money it doesn't have to be the end. The goal is to learn a lesson from any state of affairs you found was a setback in your pursuit of happiness.

7

FRIENDS

"Be weary of those who criticize you in public and
congratulate you in private."
Yusef Abdullah III

Psalm 82:6

1983

Have you ever been let down or hurt by your friends? Have you ever wondered how someone so close could betray you? Have you ever considered that they weren't friends at all? Are images of school classrooms and lunchrooms popping into your head?

Maybe it's high school and you're thinking about the people you use to hang out with. It's possible and very likely that someone in that group hurt you either then or after high school.

That was the past. Now you are older, wiser, and there is no way you are still being let down or hurt by your friends, right? Again, I'll suggest what if the people that hurt you were never your friends at all? *Hussain, that's obvious. Clearly a true friend would never hurt you.* Allow me the chance to expound on my claim.

In a previous life, I taught elementary school students general studies including reading, writing, and arithmetic (my favorite), amongst other disciplines such as art, social studies, and science. One theme that always came up was precision.

I taught during the common core era where developing critical thinking was at the forefront of the educational agenda in contrast to other generations where rote learning and memorization were the hallmarks.

No matter what your opinion is of common core studies and the politics behind the concept, the idea that in order to think critically you had to be able to be precise and use proper vocabulary terms to do so is noteworthy.

From time to time I would do a short activity with my students that highlighted the significance of being specific and detailed when you were explaining or describing something. The presentation would arise naturally like most good teaching points where I felt it was necessary for the lesson or for the students in general to be put in a situation where they could experience how the lack of quality detail and directions could cause confusion.

If I were covering a class and I noticed a lot of the students were using vague terms or one-word answers to their responses I would stop the mini lesson and use this task as a method of refocusing the group.

The majority of my 14-year career with the NYC DoE was spent as a specialist. I started off as a paraprofessional (or assistant teacher as I pursued my bachelor's degree). The principals I worked with knew my skill sets and potential, so I wasn't given the typical roles that the average paraprofessional (para) would receive.

Typically, an assistant teacher would work with one class for the year or with one teacher year in and year out, sometimes for 30 years consecutively. It happens more often than you'd think. My roles as a para were more focused on getting me ready for my time in front of the room.

One year I worked with the gifted and talented (g&t) classes from grades one to five with a sprinkle of kindergarten mixed in here and there. Every day I would bounce around for a few reasons. Sometimes I was put in a classroom because the teachers lacked classroom management.

. . .

NOW IF YOU'VE ever been in a gifted and talented classroom, you might know for a fact that although some children were able to pass an exam to get into a special education setting that the children are not any easier to manage. For those who are unclear, special education is not a place, it is a series of services including gifted and talented programs; any accommodations or special setting outside of general education is considered "special education".

Imagine how differently children and parents might feel about receiving special education services if they had this level of understating as opposed to the stereotypical notion of small buses and "slow" children.

Imagine how some arrogant parents or students might feel if they knew that they were receiving special education services. I have seen so many instances of parents not willing to give their children the tools required to allow them to succeed on or above grade level because of the stigmas associated with "being special ed".

At times, some of the best lesson planners are not the best with controlling a group. This phenomenon is typical of some other fields where the reward for being weak is an easier work load whereas your reward for excelling at your practice is a tougher work load (usually without rewards or gratitude).

· · ·

IN THOSE CASES, my assignment was necessary because two heads and four hands are better than one and two. My job was to keep the peace and to learn as much as I could about the content and teaching methods while working.

In other classrooms I was sent in as another set of hands with some strong teachers. In these cases, I was there primarily to observe how to conduct lessons, take notes, and organize my data (as those who were there know NYC teachers at that time were working under the accountability era of education).

I was being primed and set up for success by those leaders who knew that I could be a valued asset to their school communities both real time as an added bonus to these g&t teachers, the students, and their test scores, which at that time meant salary bonuses for administration.

As time passed I was also given other special assignments such as being the liaison for the swim program. Once a week my day was spent as a co chaperone to second grade students at the local YMCA for a weekly free-swimming program. I actually learned how to swim as an adult by attending this program with the children.

Even early on, I was more of a specialist than a classroom teacher in the eyes of the students. When your child has a good teacher, they light up. Students can't wait for PD 3 on Thursday when Mr. H is going to come in and continue the ongoing math project with them.

That was early on. As the years progressed I honed my skills. I saw the errors in my ways as an educator in terms of content knowledge, philosophy, management, data analysis, and so on. At the time of the pretension I will discuss next I was 10 to 12 years in, I had worked with several thousand students, and I had begun my work as a "math coach" (a staff developer who specialized in mathematics).

These details are crucial to painting the picture of an educator who can walk into a room and the class is overjoyed when said educator walks in the room. I'll also warn any rookie teachers who might try this to proceed with caution. I was a highly respected and decorated professional with a lot more leeway than most because of my success and my personality. I could pull off some things in a classroom setting that your general instructor might not be able to.

Now I'll set the stage. Imagine a group of 20 to 25 students with ages ranging from six to 11. On any given day, I could be working with a kindergarten group or a fifth-grade class.

Imagine a multi-ethnic class all wide-eyed and excited to see what today's lesson was going to be. They are sitting on a rug in designated spots. Some are just around the rug in chairs for lack of space, or as a measure of classroom management. It is five minutes into the period and we have embarked on a new teaching point.

The activity went something like this.

"Hey guys, who likes money?"

In unison, they all exclaimed, "Me, me, me, me."

I would reach into my pocket and pull out whatever I had. It could be a dollar, it could be twenty thousand; both garnered the same response with the students, to them, money was money. At that time, I was already finding success in real estate. During lunch and after work I attended closings or I had to pay for something. Other times I was just going shopping.

If I didn't have anything in my pocket, I altered the presentation. I would show them the money to get a buy in and attention. I would ask for volunteers to try and win the money. Now I am not a gambling man so I knew they had no chance in winning and they also couldn't lose anything from participating. We proceeded.

I would point to some obscure, usually cluttered (most classrooms), or multi-faceted (for those who were seriously organized) areas in the room and I would challenge my participant to retrieve an object.

If they could retrieve the object, they would win the prize. If they couldn't obtain the item they would have to give the next volunteer a turn. We would do this 2-3 times before I was accused of cheating or not being clear and that's when the exercise stopped.

Participant 1: "Grace, can you go over there and grab me the thing from the box (as I pointed far off to the back of the room). You have ten seconds."

The class usually gave the students advice or tips as they laughed and aided in the search. Grace would call back here, here, what color is it, here asking for guidance but as always, the student was unsuccessful in the scavenger hunt. "Ok Grace, come have a seat and let's try another student."

Participant 2: "Adrian, you're up next. Can you go grab me the thing from the space in the back. You have ten seconds."

He runs to the back as time is of the essence. He touched as many things as possible in a frenetic manner, trying to up his odds by adding volume to his search. The class is excited and entertained by this classroom game show, "Who wants Mr. H's money?" As always nada, nil, nothing. He was unsuccessful in his pursuit.

At this point I would stop the hunt and ask the students (if they hadn't already figured it out), "Why couldn't your classmates find the thing?"

They would usually scream at me, "Because you cheated", or "Because you didn't tell them what to find", or "You didn't tell them where it was!!"

"Oooooooooh!!!" I would say leaning back in my chair. "You mean, I wasn't being precise or specific?"

Whole class emphatically said, "YES!!"

I carry on with the conversation:

Now I see. I should have asked Grace or Adrian to bring me the green folder with the rainbow decagon (five-pointed star, did I mention I was a math teacher) at the Brooklyn table. Well that makes a lot of sense.

So today, when you are continuing your work on your volume project, estimating the size of the school, be sure to use as many details as possible in your step by step explanations, and also be sure to be as precise as possible in your measurement. Are you going to use feet, inches, meters, yards, bricks, windows? Remember, the scale counts.

ONE MORE GIFT to the parents and teachers reading this book. My lessons were open ended. No one wants to sit through 5-15 presentations of the same thing. The students were allowed to partner or work in scaffold (guided, sometimes mixed skill level and other times similar skill levels depending on all sorts of factors).

They developed their understanding. I never gave them a formula and asked them to go off and solve ten problems using the formula. That's not math. Math is about exploration. It's about problem solving and using logic to find the most efficient ways to arrive at a solution. My students were allowed to find their answers anyway they wanted to.

During that investigation I could have given them 100 problems and the formula for volume L x W x H and said solve these and give them a score. Some of you are cringing right now suffering from math based PTSD because you lived this life and some of your children are experiencing this at this very point in time. No, the key is to have fun and make real world connections. Who cares about the formula for volume?

But if you can engage the students with a question a handful of them might be interested in, like, How big is our school building? Well, now they are captivated. At first, they might think it's impossible to discover. Once they find they can actually solve such a problem, it gives them so much confidence and pleasure to have the fulfillment of succeeding and persevering at a difficult task.

You have to incorporate multiple content areas in as much of your instruction as possible. This study began with a photograph of the school and estimates based on guesses. Then, a study on scale. That was followed by a walking trip outside to search for items we could use to help us count. Some students used a fire hydrant.

They found it was 39 inches, if I recall correctly. They could count the building by fire hydrants and could create their own formulas. Others converted the fire hydrant into a standard measure, such as a meter or a yard, and then divided their answers by three (3) to measure in feet.

Other groups used windows, cars, bricks, or the concrete squares on the sidewalk. They noticed so many things from having a real experience as opposed to a dry worksheet. They all had their own photographs to work from so they could use manipulatives (tangible items) to assist with counting.

We might have students find that a die was the same size as the car in the photograph so the school building on their presentation was four (4) dice tall and seven (7) dice wide. This was learning at its finest. I was having fun and engaged; the children were having fun and engaged.

My onlookers (typically, when I taught lessons I would have new teachers or veteran teachers shadow my work as a form of collaborative professional development) were having fun and engaged. This is how learning should take place. For all educators out there, let the students drive the instruction. The days of the "sage on the stage" are gone.

If you go back and look at that flashback to my time in the classroom you might notice something. I never used the words friend or friends during my discussions involving the children interacting or my work with my adult counterparts.

As someone who was paid to teach the significance of such ideas as detail and precision it would only be correct if I followed suit in my own life. When someone uses the word "friend" you have a very different image in your head than if they'd selected the terms classmate, coworker, church member, teammate.

As you read the list you might have had images of people you know pop into your head or others who fit your "schema" for those terms. Behavioral psychologist, Jean Piaget, believed a schema has two parts: the understanding of the item in question and the continuous development of that item over time. Meaning as you continue to have experiences you continue to refine your view of the schema.

One of the most famous examples, something you might have experienced with your own child, is the schema for a dog. Depending on their early experience, anything furry with a tail is a dog. They see a cat, they say dog. They see a raccoon, they say dog.

Over time they learn the character traits of a dog

and other similar animals, and begin to create new schemas for each animal, modifying their previous understandings. These modifications take place as new experiences and learning take place.

The takeaway from this piece of behavioral psychology is that it is related to our feelings about our friends. The term is grossly overused. Think about it for a moment. Have you ever been out at a bar or at a conference? You're there with your family, friends, or coworkers and someone walks over to you. They recognize you before you notice them.

They excitedly say, "Hey, how are you?!! Oh my God, it's been forever!" They might or might not know your name or visa versa.

You both know it and you begin the awkward introductions, "Mom, Dad this friend..." You pause, he bails you out. Hi I'm Steve. He goes in for the handshake. You think to yourself, "Oh yea Steve, that's right, from sophomore year in undergrad."

The awkward interview resumes, "How have you been? What have you been up to these past ten years? Are you married now?"

Five minutes later you're following one another on social media and this person you know nothing about gets to see your wife in a bikini from your trip to Puerto Rico, and your new car because your private page is now fully accessible all because you used the "F" word. This is someone you didn't know fifteen minutes earlier, now you're following someone with opposing political views who tags you on posts with offensive jokes and even worse possibly connects you with other people from college you've tried to distance yourself from.

Maybe it wasn't an old college classmate, perhaps it was sometime on your team from peewee baseball. Whatever the connection, they weren't your friends then but they are now? It could be that you were friends during peewee baseball and you've reconnected some twenty years later at the mall or taking public transportation.

What I want you to consider is, what made you friends? You were six years old. At age six anyone who has candy or toys to share is the best person in the world.

Think back to the old neighborhood. You had a group of friends. Where I'm from, we called it our crew. You have your crew of friends. You're all from the same building (remember I'm from Brooklyn, I grew up in a 38-unit building) or from the same block. Maybe you shared the same corner.

In my teens I hung out on 8th St. in Brighton Beach. My friends all pretty much lived on 8th St. We weren't the only kids on 8th St. There were different crews. At that time, we all had different interests. My crew were mostly athletes.

No other crew in our neighborhood could beat us at

any sport. There were other crews: some sold drugs, others did drugs. Some were more focused on school or other things.

The point I'm making is that my friends at the time were my friends because of three factors: age, proximity, and a common thread. We were all teens, our age gap four years, top to bottom. That range existed because of siblings. We all had ties to 8th St., so we had our corner and finally, we liked sports, girls, and had similar goals. We all wanted money, jewelry, clothes, and, well, girls.

In my preteen years my friends were from a different part of Brooklyn called Park Slope. I went to grammar and middle school there. My friends there were all from "9th Ave" (as we called it); to those of you not from the old Park Slope, Prospect Park West.

My elementary school had students in it from 4th Ave up to 9th Ave. My classmates were all from 7th Ave and below. So, I had my school friends and my after-school friends.

My school friends were made up of a collective that had age, intelligence (at that point classes were tracked and based on aptitude; I was in a Level One (1) class that meant we were the smartest) and again, proximity. In elementary, generally speaking, you attended your neighborhood school. My neighborhood didn't have good schools, so my mom (a school teacher) made sure I went to the schools in her district.

. . .

LOOKING BACK on these different groupings I've noticed and remembered that within those groups there were lots of different dynamics. We all had little groups within the groups. There were always tandems and triplets within the larger collective groups or crews. I always remember having one or two really close friends within my circle of friends and a few friends that I really never liked. I would never call them or hang out with them purposely.

An example would be going to the park. When the weather got nice in Brooklyn the schoolyard was the place to be. We would play ball all day, every day. Early morning on Saturday around 10 or 11 we would meet at the park; maybe at the corner store on the way to the park or just at the park.

The first thing I did on a Saturday was get up, get dressed, and head to 253 (a local elementary school playground) or go straight to Grady (a local high school with the best court and competition in the neighborhood). Sometimes I would warm up at 253 or head to Grady with two to three people so when we got there we could run threes or at least have a team for a full court game.

Sometimes I would get to Grady and shoot around with someone from my crew I didn't like. But if anything should happen we were friends so we had one another's back. It's kind of like siblings. You can call your brother or sister anything as a child but no one else can.

Now fast forward to our current date in time and think about social media. Generations past never had to encounter the awkwardness of a friend request or a follow from an undesirable.

Didn't these people get the message back in '96? Our relationship has run its course. '96-'98 we had our time. Fate had it set up where after graduation we never had to see each other ever again now I have to accept your friend request because we have fifteen mutual friends?

You send me a request to a private page. I accept it; you don't say hello, you don't like or comment on a post, but you watch every story I share like a season finale, and this is all done because of the interactions we had as children. I disagree. It's time for another "F" word. It's time to "F" it. You guessed it correctly! Now is the perfect time to F.E.A.R.

This reset will begin with a new level of attention to detail. We are going to adjust our schemas; and, as a toddler does when categorizing four legged animals and begins to tease apart attributes, so shall we. If we went to school together we were "classmates". If we played a sport together we were "teammates". We worked together; we were "coworkers", "colleagues", or "workmates".

Some designations are a bit more complex and require another word or two. Here are phrases you can use to describe some other individuals you might have come into contact with over the years, my "mechanic", "a former business partner", my "CPA", my "dentist". You should always try to use someone's name when referring to them in an introductory scenario. If this is someone who is undesirable why are you speaking about them at all?

When you see people in different designated groups, it makes it much easier to decipher. The sentence *I can't believe that the kid I grew up with twenty years ago cheated me out of $500* sounds very different than, *My friend stole $500 from me.*

Let's try a couple more. *I cannot believe she had sex with my husband. I knew her from age 6 to age 10 and we haven't spoken until we recently reconnected on social media after a fifteen-year hiatus.* That story sounds extremely likely when compared to *How could my childhood friend have an affair with my husband?*

F.E.A.R let it all go. I am not saying you cannot have friends that you have made along the way. I am saying that I have a core group of people that I stay connected to as much as possible. We hit it off when we met. We have had ups and downs, we have mutual interests, and we enjoy one another's company. We also have mutual respect. With those key components lined up we can call one another friend or family.

Too often people are hurt by those they give too much credit to based on fleeting forced conditions. If you didn't like someone back in third grade chances are you're not going to like them in your thirties; it's ok to ignore the "follow" request.

If there is someone you'd like to reconnect with from twenty years ago by all means you should do so. My fiancé and wife to be (possibly by the time this book comes out, pending COVID-19) reconnected on social media in the most improbable of ways. That story might make it into this book, it might not, we shall see.

The key takeaway is, are you happy? When you wake up in the morning can you say I'm happy with where I am in life? I'm where I want to be or I'm on the road to pursuing that destination.

If the answer is yes, then you more than likely agree with my statements because you have done so in your life already.

If your answer is no, you might want to start changing your environment by taking a critical inventory of those individuals around you currently.

If your current core group doesn't motivate you, doesn't support you, doesn't wish you well, or doesn't offer you anything in that relationship it's time to move on. Sever ties. You don't have to be mean or cold you just have to begin to create space for yourself and put distance between you and the other party. You will find the distance will grow on its own quite naturally.

As you find new success, if you allow them to stay connected via social media or via email or cell, have no doubt that those connections will allow a bridge to form allowing them access to your new-found success and new relationships will form. Not one born out of friendship, but one born out of all the wrong ingredients and that relationship will most certainly end in a negative way.

Once you begin to ascend and others who cannot rise with you see that ascent, the feelings of entitlement and resentment will begin to set in. Remember you do not owe anyone anything. Help those who deserve it, not those who seek it. There is a difference.

If someone cannot contribute something financially but they are willing to learn and do the work required to build together, they are an ally. Keep them around. If someone has the means, but doesn't want to do the work, they can be an investor but keep them at arm's length. If someone doesn't want to contribute, move on and don't look back. If they come back into your life they can be a client, at best.

Keep your loved ones close and protect those relationships as if you were protecting gold. Any other relationships, keep at a distance. You do not have to like everyone you encounter as long as they serve a purpose. You can have mutual respect without liking someone. You cannot have friendship with dislike.

We have limited time on this Earth; don't waste your precious moments with anyone who doesn't deserve them.

8

LEADERSHIP

"A leader is one who knows the way, goes the way and shows the way."
John C Maxwell

Grandpa

2002

What makes a leader a leader? What image just popped in your head? Was it your "boss"? Maybe a terrible supervisor, current or previous? Maybe it was a great leader, someone world renowned for their excellence in mobilizing others. Whoever you imagined I want you to ask yourself was that person truly a leader?

·   ·   ·

HAVE you ever heard the saying, "Man makes the money, money doesn't make the man"? Let's break that saying down and align it with leaders and leadership. At times, we correlate income or wealth with leadership.

In my estimation, your salary or net worth does not qualify you as one who can motivate others to achieve one common goal. "Man makes the money" simply means you can earn any dollar amount minuscule or major. "Money doesn't make the man" is the key for our discussion.

What might be obvious to some, on the surface, may not be so clear to your subconscious. We attribute power to the rich. How the person in question made their money doesn't matter but it should. For the scope of this conversation, I will stereotype a bit and say that usually if we are presented with a figure, they are automatically granted courage, brains, and a heart, as if they walked the yellow brick road in Oz to achieve their success.

In the '90s and early 2000s we could look at a celebutante like Paris Hilton. She inherited $300 million dollars as an inheritance from her family namesake, the Hilton Hotel franchise. She was born rich and was given opportunities that allowed her to go from being an unknown to an influencer.

There are other people with more skills and intelligence, but they do not have the same access in the market. She was dubbed a genius by some because she capitalized on her fame and created an "empire" by becoming a brand.

In my estimation, turning $300 million into $500 million is a very easy feat. Starting off at the finish line and completing a marathon does not make you an athlete. This is not a criticism of her personally. The point that we have to focus on here is that she was looked at as a success and as a guru to some.

Her time in the spotlight was the precursor to the Kardashian phenomenon we are currently in the midst of. Kim Kardashian's reign as the latest celebutante was born the same as her predecessor. They both gained fame from having sex tapes leaked to the masses as a tool to gain them attention, whether purposely or accidentally.

Kris Jenner is usually attributed as the brains behind the Kardashian /Jenner machine, even though Kim, Kylie and the others have their own lanes and currently Kim is using her voice to impact social injustices. Again, taking advantage of this notoriety and capitalizing on it does not make you good or bad. It also shouldn't make you intelligent or unintelligent.

On a general level we would likely agree that someone's bank account doesn't make them a good or a bad person although there are stigmas that are associated with wealth and poverty.

. . .

I RECENTLY HAD a family friend tell me "Don't make too much money, people with money are usually bad people." She was as serious as a heart attack. She is someone who holds multiple degrees. Professionally, she worked in education for decades and she herself is a multi-millionaire.

Now to clarify, she inherited a valuable piece of property in the Brooklyn Heights neighborhood, Downtown, Brooklyn, NY. This property alone is currently worth close to $2,000,000 if not more. She then added pieces to her real estate portfolio leveraging this property to add to her lifestyle, not her wealth. What that means to her is, she isn't adding to her income.

Her mindset is that she is living a modest lifestyle as a retiree yet, her game plan for her next investment was to "sell the condo in Florida and sell the house in Asbury (New Jersey) to buy an apartment in the city (Manhattan)". She wanted to take all of her wealth to have an apartment in one of the most expensive cities in the world.

I explained how if she took the same money and invested in a small city that could use an infusion of fresh investors that she could make 10 times the income. She could have the same apartment, and use her extra income to give back to the community in form of donations and scholarships but she has such a negative view on capitalists and capitalism.

Her response was, "No I'd prefer to just have my apartment, it's a better investment."

In her mind she doesn't see herself as a millionaire because she is not a business minded person. Her wealth rests in properties she lives in mixed with her pension. By definition, she is a multimillionaire. She may not have accrued her net wealth in sales or production yet she is still far from impoverished.

When I pointed this out to her as we spoke about her comment she instantly had to end the call. This was her exact statement almost verbatim, "Oh my God a dolphin just swam past my window! I have to go get my camera. I'll speak to you soon." And she hung up.

Is she a leader? Is Paris or Kim? Is LeBron? Is Trump? These questions might be easy for some and hard for others to answer. In order to answer this question about those just mentioned or for anyone else we have to set agreed upon parameters.

So, again I'll ask what makes a leader a leader? Merriam Webster believes a leader is "someone who leads a group". Thanks folks, that is groundbreaking stuff. Dictionary.com suggests a leader is, "a person or thing that leads." Again, mind blowing depth here.

Sarcasm aside for a moment, if the sources we go to for specificity on defining terms are vague, there is no wonder why we attribute the power and gravitas that should be reserved for true leaders to anyone who has an inkling of authority. Let's continue to break this down.

For those of you who choose to use this term, I implore you to cease after reading this paragraph. Let's start with the title, "boss". Do you have a boss? I've never had a boss in my life and I never will.

Let's see what Merriam-Webster has to say about this noun, "boss: a person who exercises control or authority". I'll wait... Does your "boss", "exercise control and authority" over you? If you can answer yes to that question, I want you to stop and think about what you are feeling after answering yes to that question. This might be an opportune time to enact F.E.A.R.

I have worked with people who were clearly not as capable, not as intelligent, not as experienced, or not as worthwhile as I was in certain parts of my career. There is a common joke (remember I was in formal education for 14 years and my mother was a teacher) that says, "Those who can't do, teach"; maybe you've heard it. Within education, the addition to that joke is, "Those who can't teach, become administrators."

There are a multitude of ways to take that saying. You can look at it as a progression such as when an athlete can no longer compete on the court or the field they step over to the sideline and coach. Or you can interpret the saying as perhaps someone who never had the ability to become an athlete, yet understood a sport, was a coach from the beginning.

I don't see the saying as a direct shot at educators or teachers who want to help kindergarteners learn to read. It might apply, and in my career it certainly did, in some cases. For example, I have worked with failed writers who decided to take a job as a literacy teacher because they wanted the flexibility of the schedule and the benefits that come with a union job. Those types of teachers give the profession a bad name.

As far as administration goes, the concept of a principal began as a master teacher who earned their stripes being put in a situation to serve as a support for new and veteran teachers. In my experience, the role of principal or administrator became a golden ticket out of the classroom. There were people who wanted to become principals specifically.

They had no interest in education, they were more interested in becoming the boss. At the time I was in the classroom, several fast-track to administration programs were created where non-educators, and even those with three years of experience could apply and be hired as administrators.

This was a terrible time for education. In fact, Betsy Devos, President Trump's choice for the national head of education, had no education experience at all. This climate was detrimental to education as a whole.

That is not to say that the Trump administration is responsible for all the ills that education faced; however, it is a direct example of how someone can be deemed a leader, supervisor, boss, or authority over something and not be equipped or worthy of a title or a designation.

In my estimation, YOU have a direct supervisor: a supervisor is "one that supervises". To truly digest this definition that Merriam-Webster provides, we have to define supervise. What does supervise mean?Merriam-Webster offers this explanation, "to be in charge of" also see oversee and superintend.

My belief is, there is power in words. If you believe you are being "supervised" by a "boss" and you were taught that this structure is acceptable, I'd like you to consider the source of your information. I would also like you to reconsider the information you now give to your children and their children in terms of social and economic structures.

How can a child born into poverty feel equal or adequate when their pursuit of happiness has to go through institutions that champion getting a job and having a boss that will supervise them and oversee their production? Is that what you want your children to believe? Is that the truth?

Do you require an overseer "to watch over and direct (an undertaking, a group of workers, etc.) in order to ensure a satisfactory outcome or performance" (Merriam-Webster online dictionary)? If that is the case you might want to think about why you feel the need to have someone "above" you for you to complete your daily professional tasks.

For the rest of us why not use a term like "team leader"? Let's look into those words.

Team: a number of persons associated together in work or activity (Merriam-Webster online dictionary).

Leader: a person who leads; see guide or conductor.

Doesn't that sound so much more inviting? Wouldn't you prefer to go into your place of business (not your "job" we have to F.E.A.R that term as well) as a member of a team where your coach or leader is there to guide you in one common goal?

In all of my different business ventures, I do not have workers or employees. I have partners, contractors and vendors. We are all a team, no one is above another. I am not paying a subservient person. I am paying a contractor for a service.

The office that garners our company name is a work site no different than the addresses of the homes we renovate. Everyone is their own "BOSS" we are all accountable for our own wellbeing, yet we are not alone. We are all equally important pieces in a unified front all working towards one common goal.

. . .

THERE ARE no such things as good or bad leaders. You are either a leader or not. Whether you are born that way or you are groomed into one that is a discussion for another day. In my estimation a leader has integrity, humility, accountability, a specific set of skills required for the work presented, and they have the trust of the team.

The leader should be one who might not be the "smartest" or the strongest, maybe they aren't the senior person on the project. The leader should be the person who can get the group to the promised land efficiently and effectively. They should be the person that gets the best from the group and can maintain high morale.

At times, I am a leader, in other situations I am led. That is fine and always acceptable. Being overseen and supervised will never be tolerated.

If you are not a leader, look at that short list in the previous paragraph and do the work to check all of those items off of your list unless you are comfortable with being a follower. Do not make the mistake of believing leaders can't be led. We can all be leaders in our own right.

Remember, steer clear of those who are never wrong, but are always wronged. Leaders and successful people do not pass the buck or make excuses. They always look for their part in any negative interaction in the pursuit of being their best selves. They are apologetic and reflective.

If you always feel like a victim or as if things are always in your way in order for you to fail, you are the true obstacle. F.E.A.R and get out of your own way.

9

BINGO

"The worst guilt is to accept an unearned guilt."
Ayn Rand

Shape Bingo Game Box
2015

As of March 2020, there are currently an estimated 2.3 million prisoners being held in some form of prison. Each year over 600,000 Americans enter prison gates and over 10.6 million are sent to jail. The difference between jail and prison is, you can be sent to jail and detained while still innocent.

. . .

PEOPLE WHO CANNOT AFFORD bond have to stay in jail until their court date. Those who have been convicted or plead guilty are sentenced to prison to serve their time. Ninety-five percent of felony convictions are obtained by a guilty plea.

In the case of the five teens from New York City known previously as the "Central Park 5", and now known as the "Exonerated 5", these young men were forced into serving between 6 and 13 years individually, all due to a corrupt and broken justice system that disproportionately affects poor black and brown males.

Why and how do you ask? Because they chose to fight the system, they were chewed up and spat out. The oldest member of the group, then 16-year-old Corey Wise, was sentenced as an adult. He was mentally disabled and was not even at the scene of the crime. He went with his friend to the precinct so he wouldn't be alone.

For those of you who haven't ever been in a situation where the chips are stacked against you, I ask you to complete this chapter before you ask, "Why would someone plead guilty to something they didn't do?" Before I had the experience I am going to expound on, I had the arrogance and privilege of asking such a question.

On February 16th, 2018, I admitted to (I'll paraphrase; this is a public record so you can read the court document if you'd like) being an employee of the New York City Department of Education since 2010. I had to admit that I was a city employee to establish my stance as a public servant.

Next, I had to agree that at some point between 2015 and 2017, I used work time to demonstrate and market a product called "Shape Bingo" that I intended to sell online for personal profit. The next part digs deeper into the specifics of what took place during the two year period.

This includes demonstrating the game at a staff workshop, asking a teacher to "launch" the game on YouTube, and selling a copy of the game to a teacher in October of 2016. The final part of the agreement states, "I represent that I did not make profit from the geometry bingo."

I had to agree that I used city time to make a personal profit, commonly known as "double dipping"; being paid by a job and making money while being on the clock. My penalty for this admission: $1,000. The check was made out to the City of New York, Conflicts of Interest Board (or COIB).

Hussain, why would you pay $1,000 for something you didn't do? Obviously you weren't guilty. I'll state the facts, and you can be the judge. Or rather, the board. The COIB hearings do not have a judge. Your fate is determined by a panel of people. It is a court, but it is not what you see on television.

As I mentioned previously in the book, I worked for a Fortune 500 company in a corporate tower in the Midwest. I made more money than I knew what to do with as an 18-year-old kid from the inner city. I worked at this company because the money was great. I had everything I could want.

At the time, I had a poor person's mindset. Again, I'd like to remind you about CLK (Chapter Seven). CLK was a signed and sealed millionaire. She had over $1,000,000.00 in her bank account. With that, she still had a poor person's mindset, and as you saw from her story, she squandered that money as you would expect someone who has a poor person's mentality to do.

Rich and poor mindsets have nothing to do with how much money you have in the bank, or how much money you earn. It has to do with how you see, earn, and spend your capital.

Now, I was poor so I believed trading time for money was a winning proposition. I worked every hour of overtime I could. I loved those checks. The job was easy. The money was great and I felt like a million bucks.

One day we had an opportunity to volunteer with a well-known nationwide program where adults mentor young men and women, almost like siblings. I jumped at

the opportunity, and when my time came for the culmi-
nation of the mentorship, I showed up to the junior high
school and met my assigned student. We were allowed
to take the full day off of work with pay in exchange for
volunteering for two hours.

Most of the other volunteers showed up late, left
early, and took cigarette breaks during the time we were
supposed to be volunteering. I ended up having a better
day than I had at work in a long time. I stayed until the
end of lunch, and ended up hanging out with a group of
the young men who were supposed to be mentored
that day.

Now that I think about it, imagine how excited to
meet my young mentee I had to be to bring a camera to
the school to meet the young man I had sent letters back
and forth with as a part of the program.

I felt a breath of fresh air. I made it very clear that I had no intention of attending college after school. I also made it clear that my lack of a plan led to my being sent to the Midwest, *Fresh Prince* style. Just about two years earlier, prior to my high school graduation I had the privilege of doing my internship at my elementary school alma mater.

Some of my teachers were still there. They were so proud of my growth and my choice to pursue education. They also knew my mom as she taught across the street at a middle school I would later attend.

I got to work in the computer lab with one of the coolest teachers I ever had whom we shall call Mr. Ninja. He showed me so many things during my high school internship. My coursework was only 40 hours. I remember doing almost double the time because I loved working with the children so much. During my teens I also used to volunteer to referee the peewee games at the local gym before our teen games so they could play.

If no one was there to referee, their games were cancelled. I would show up an hour before some games just to make sure they had the chance to have fun. There is something about education that elicits an emotional experience I cannot describe in words. It might be genetic as both my mother and father were teachers. My mother, for the city, as a junior high school health teacher and my father as a martial arts instructor.

After leaving that middle school and hanging out with those young men I knew what I had to do so I signed up for a local community college and began my course to become a teacher. At the time I was making more than a new teacher would make in New York City, and way more than a teacher would make in Minneapolis. At age 20 this was one of the first times

F.E.A.R took place in my decision making. I knew then money wasn't more important than happiness.

Northeast Middle School
Minneapolis, MN
2002

As I am writing this I also just had an epiphany or an "aha moment". What kind of foresight and wisdom must my mother have had to see that I would end up making the right choices given the opportunity to figure things out on my own? She entrusted me with my 30-year-old cousin in a city well over 1,000 miles away. She never forced college or the military on me.

She just sent me away like Angela Bassett did her son Tre in the 1991 classic movie Boyz N The Hood. She said, "I can't teach Tre how to be a man. That's your job." She sends Tre to live with his dad Furios Styles, played by Laurence Fishburne. Fishburne coincidentally attended the junior high school I attended.

I ended up moving back to New York City before I could attend college so I signed up for Brooklyn College (BC), a local university. I had a relationship with BC as I was a high school student on the campus school, Brooklyn College Academy (BCA).

My career path was set. I worked for the city full time and went to school full time as well as coached basketball, held a second job as an after school counselor, and ran a graphic design and printing business.

Initially, I set out to work with junior high school students. Anyone in education can tell you junior high school is the toughest population to work with outside of kindergarten. Every kindergarten teacher should get paid an extra 10% of whatever the teaching salary is.

That year of school is the most critical in our education system as it currently stands or stood depending on how things look post COVID-19. I wanted to be a guidance counselor. Now in New York at the time there were only one or two of those jobs per building and those spots were held for many, many years.

So I did the math and thought about what else I love. I knew I didn't want to teach just to get a job. That is the fastest way to become disgruntled. I wanted to help children like myself when I was a student; a B+ student who could get A+ grades if I cared about school.

School was a fashion show and a social space for me. The classes were like the commercials between my favorite television shows. I also believe that middle school is where you become who you are.

In elementary school you have the same teacher all day and you have the same classmates all day. You are sheltered. Once you get to middle school the safety nets are removed. You go to classes by yourself. You meet new people from different schools.

That's where you get into your social group. You either play sports, or you like girls, or clothes, you try drugs for the first time, you begin to cut school or you are really into your studies, or chess or computers. Whatever it is, junior high school allows you the opportunities to explore what you wish. Those choices affect your high school, which affects your post school lifestyle.

I decided I would teach mathematics. I loved numbers and I knew it was a subject most students hated. If I could make math accessible it would be the best gift I could give to the world. So I pursued mathematics and psychology. The plan was to get a degree, teach at a middle school, and get a master's degree in counseling. Once a counseling job became available, I would transition over.

That is not exactly how it went. I ended up as an assistant teacher which shifted my licensure. I couldn't get my internship hours done at a junior high school because my work schedule was a conflict. I decided to pursue elementary education and then I would go back and get my counseling degree.

Nope! As things lined up, that wasn't the best choice either, due to a hiring freeze. I ended up thinking with the climate in education as volatile as it is, coupled with the fact that most elementary school teachers nationwide are not qualified to teach mathematics, it was the most logical career path to pursue. Some people attended the class because if you had a specialized background in a hard-to-staff field you could get hired.

I remember a large portion of my undergraduate cohort failing and dropping their matriculation because they couldn't pass the sixth-grade level math class, I also remember the ones who did stick with it cheating on midterms and finals. It got to the point in the class where my professor asked me to take the final at a different date and time so no one would cheat off of my exam.

.   .   .

I ENDED up taking the final in his office with him there and I finished in about 10 minutes. I could be just another good math teacher and affect one grade or I could become a star elementary school math teacher and affect a whole school or district.

I ended up pursuing elementary mathematics as a graduate degree and became a staff developer. I excelled in my program so much so that my professor told me I couldn't do a computation-based action research project (our equivalent to a graduate school thesis). She said challenge yourself.

You already have a strong base in mathematics (of my 15 or so cohort I had already been teaching and working in schools for years, I had been to every math training you can imagine and I had a knack for mathematics naturally).

I said I know what I'll do to challenge myself. I'll do a geometry project. I'll put together a 1-6 grade curriculum that teaches all of the Common Core Learning Standards (CCLS) in Geometry without computation. I'll teach the whole curriculum with games and activities. The idea was meant to be a challenge.

When I issued the challenge, I wasn't sure if it could even be done. My grade wasn't important. I was a shoe in for passing the class and the action research wasn't about passing an exam; it was about being thorough in the research process.

I followed suit. I developed a handful of games and activities that could be taught as a unit of study or as a center activity for small group instruction. One of those games was called "Shape Bingo".

At the time it was just something that was already in the marketplace but not done as in-depth as what I had planned and aligned to the CCLS. If you were to google Shape Bingo right now you would see 2-dimensional shapes with primary colors on a 2 x 2 or a 3 x 3 grid.

We added and patented our game with items that included non-shapes convex (all points are outward) and concave (some corners are inward). For example, a 5-pointed star is really a convex decagon as it has 10 straight sides that do not cross one another, it has 10 corners and it is a closed shape. Now if your head hurts, blame your mathematics instructors.

I taught this in kindergarten and all of the students were able to grasp it. Did I teach them the terms convex and concave? No, absolutely not. By second grade they got the terminology in alignment with the grade level standards.

This was just a game that I created for a college project in 2010. It sat in a box until 2016. At this point I was a mathematics coach and I was giving a presentation on geometry. Teachers hate to teach geometry.

There are no tools out there compared to what you can find for addition and multiplication. You actually have to plan it out and create your own content. This is extremely difficult when you do not have the proper training. This is not the fault of the teacher. This is the fault of the licensure process.

Elementary school teachers have to take one course in mathematics that has maybe two days at best that cover geometry. The course doesn't speak to shape definitions or anything else required to teach in a classroom. At that time, there were 10 courses you have to take to matriculate: one (1) science, one (1) math, and the other eight (8) are literacy based.

It is no wonder children spend most of the day reading and writing when the standard is supposed to include much more math and science. Compared globally, this is the reason the United States consistently has some of the worst performance in math and sciences.

After my presentation I gave the teachers in the workshop a copy of the game. They took photographs and we had a good time. A veteran among the teachers suggested that I package and sell the game. I thought it was a good idea. This is the crux of the whole court case.

I agreed to the statements that I marketed and used company time to develop a game. The posts that were made on social media, the emails, and my college records all show that this game was created years before the workshop, and before I had any intent to package and sell the game.

The specific event that led to the court case was the devious plotting of some teachers who were in the process of being fired and an administrator who had a vendetta. I was placed in a precarious situation by malicious and cowardly people. I was called into a classroom and specifically asked about my game.

At the time, I had a website and a tutoring business that shared the same name and brand as the company that published this very book. I never sold any games in the building nor did I ever tutor a student or a family member who was attending any building I was assigned to.

The person who was coerced to testify against me had a nephew who was struggling in mathematics. I told her I couldn't help her as a tutor. I did give her a gift. I gave her a copy of the game and a t-shirt for her nephew. She offered to take me to lunch for the favor. I said no need to do that. I was glad to help.

She then told one of her friends about the gift. Her friend was the same woman who suggested I should sell the game. Again, this was a teacher who was being forced out of the door due to lack of performance. This teacher befriended an administrator who was not fond of me as I was the building's union chapter leader and I had taken her to task on several counts of unprofessional and non-contractual requests.

This retaliatory action was an act of union animus on the part of the administrator and the teacher. Both of which were on their way out of education because of their track records while I was winning awards and being nominated for the most prodigious teaching award in the city: the Big Apple Award. I was a finalist out of over 100,000 possible contestants that same year. My credentials and skills had never been questioned.

The teacher that received the gift was reported to the administrator and was threatened into testifying. She was told that if she didn't testify that she would be fired and would face civil penalties. She acted as Corey Wise did, faced with interrogation after interrogation, about six interviews in total. She finally said the game was sold to her after being shown a text message of her admitting to having the game.

The same message she sent to her friend. Ask yourself, why would someone ask you to speak to someone about something specific then text you about it after seeing you the same day. Why did it have to be in writing?

With the word of an eye witness and several other statements it was my word against several others. Now the accounts of the other teachers were not accusatory, they were merely statements that were strewn together to tell a narrative. This was not a criminal case so the weight of the evidence is not held to the reasonable doubt criteria. It is enough to have an accusation and a foundation as this is a private institution.

I couldn't wait to say my piece. The union that represented me thought otherwise. I was wisely told by my union not to speak. What my union knew at that point that I didn't was that this was not going to end within the department of education. They knew that anything I said during my preliminary investigation would end up at another office in the city, the COIB. So I had to stay quiet.

It was one of the toughest things I had to do. The way the karmic powers of the universe would have it this court case ended up being one of the best things that ever happened to me.

If you remember a few paragraphs back, I described my schedule as a teen and as a young adult. I always worked, volunteered, played sports, and had businesses. I am still the same today.

The beauty of this court case was that it forced me to slow down and concentrate. At the time things were picking up, Shape Bingo had begun to take off with sales. I had speaking engagements lined up. My tutoring business had continued to grow.

Real estate was exploding. I was driving a new BMW and wearing a presidential Rolex to work. I even began developing the Shape Bingo App. You can still download the demo version of "Mind Molders Shape Bingo" on the Google Play store to this day.

People hated me. Could you imagine if some young, smart, and confident person came around seemingly flaunting their success? You are a veteran in the same field and you haven't accomplished half of what this person did and they had done it "matter of factly"?

Most people would despise a person with such gifts, if they were struggling. I fell into Shape Bingo; it wasn't a lifelong dream. At that point in my career I already had a foot out the door of formal education. My real estate business at the time made me more money than I could ever make as a teacher, coupled with the tutoring business, and my other investments.

The blessing in disguise was I had to shut down Mind Molders for the time being. I informed all of my tutors that they could keep 100% of their tutoring rates as homage for their good work. I shut down the Mind-molders.org website. I stopped selling merch, games, and spending time on developing the Mind Molders Shape Bingo application. I got back the gift of time. A huge weight was lifted off of my shoulders. F.E.A.R instantly struck.

I spent less time focusing on any additional or extra curricular activities around education. I did not sign up for any supplemental clubs, teams, or overtime. I resigned from everything. If you worked in that building, from the outside looking in, it possibly seemed like I was cracking under the pressure.

I know for many of my friends they thought I was stressed and the court case was taking its toll. Hopefully now they will be able to see the reality of the situation. All I did was let the inmates run the asylum. If people wanted me out of the way I gave them the opportunity to show what they could do.

The already failing school took a turn for the worst. It was hard to imagine things could get worse but they did. I was often asked if I cared about the students and if I did then why didn't I give the school my best? The answer was simple. My daughter needed me more than these other children did. I wasn't going to let anyone threaten her lifestyle. I had to spend my time securing her present and future. I decided to put my focus where it would benefit her.

The fact is I wasn't in charge of the school. I couldn't fix the problems that were simple fixes. I knew by stepping back the issues the building had would compound. I felt that would be best for the students. The parents who were aware of the deficiencies pulled their students out of the school. Others didn't but the district stepped in and added resources to the space to ensure their students were not going to fall too far behind.

As I mentioned before, I had a third college experience. I was able to get a certification as a district leader. I had to take one more test to become a principal. I knew the ins and outs of the office. I wanted no parts of it. I knew how the dominoes would fall if I let nature take its course. So I did.

During this time the case and the charges were deemed "founded"; again, this wasn't a criminal case so there was no guilt or innocence. Founded in this setting was the equivalent to being indicted by a grand jury. Now it was time to get a lawyer. Things got serious.

I wasn't dealing with principals, I was dealing with city officials. I had an appointed lawyer by the union. This lawyer was nice and honest. So honest, in fact, that she shared in her 10-12 year career (at the time) she had never once stepped into a courtroom to defend a client.

I was told that the COIB assumes that anyone who has a charge made against them has some guilt otherwise they wouldn't be in the room. Statistically, (and this is based off of several conversations over years) well over 90% of the cases that are brought against COIB are lost.

The city never loses. My union said they lose 98% of the cases they fight against this institution. They also told me that the court punished people for wasting their time. In other words, having the audacity to fight for their name.

· · ·

I HEARD all of that and I still wanted to have my day in court. I wasn't going to admit to anything that I didn't do. Then I saw my paperwork.

I had four counts against me. Each count could come with up to a $25,000 penalty. I was looking at a $100,000 penalty if I went to court to fight this case. My lawyer suggested I take a plea. She shared some stories about other clients. One woman went to her school, hired students to help her bake, and then sold her baked goods to the students and staff. She had a $250 penalty after her plea.

I was accused of selling a $20 board game one time. What were they going to charge me, $0.50? I told her to see what the plea deal was.

They came back with $1,000. At first thought I felt railroaded. How could this happen? I have to pay $1,000 for an alleged $20 sale? This is ridiculous. I was punished for the success of my business.

F.E.A.R kicked in almost instantaneously. All of those questions spiraled through my head within a split second. I literally laughed and took out about $8,000 and asked, "Do they take cash?"

It was a win for me. In life my friends and I do not take losses. We have wins and lessons. In life as an adult, lessons cost you money. When we learn a lesson, we call it tuition to business school. At that time $1,000 was the price of a sweater or aftermarket sneakers. I got off with a lesson. The city got their win and the world kept turning.

The last thing I got as a part of my plea deal was I got to admit to whatever I wanted. The charges that were brought against me are not public record. They tried to make it seem like I was Milton Bradley over a $20 board game.

I was set to retire next year. Real estate has hit new levels and being able to focus has allowed me to see things clearly. There is a silver lining in everything, all you have to do to see it is F.E.A.R.

10

PURPOSE

"God's purpose is more important than our plans."
Myles Munroe

Baby Bear and Papa Bear
on the Wonder Wheel
2011

Throughout this book you will read and discover a collection of momentous events that caused paradigm shifts in my thoughts and actions. F.E.A.R was and always is a choice.

Sometimes the situations that create these opportunities for growth are obvious to us in real time and others are in hindsight. No moment has been as glaringly apparent to F.E.A.R as the first day I met an "Angel".

As we grow up, we find that things that were the focal point of our days no longer cross our minds. The less significant the item, the more fleeting the thoughts. For most people the item at the forefront of their existence is money.

"Money makes the world go round", "Cash Rules Everything Around Me", "Get rich or die trying". These are popular phrases and mantras among ages, races and social classes. The reality is that money doesn't equal happiness.

Money is a tool like any other instrument known to man. It is only as useful as the conductor wielding it. Money however is not to be sought. Instead happiness should be your objective. The road to happiness is called your purpose. Your "why". The reason you wake up in the morning. The thing that makes you tick.

What makes you smile? What makes your day change from bad to good with a thought? Do you believe it is money? That's ok because I used to think so too until I started making it and realized otherwise. Let's try something, an exercise, if you will. Let's have a brief discussion.

HA: "What is your purpose in life?"

Bill: "Money."

HA: "Ok Bill. If you woke up tomorrow morning

with $100,000,000 in your bank account what would you do?"

Bill: "I would go shopping!!"

HA: "What would you buy?"

Bill: "I would buy a new house, a new car. I would buy some new clothes."

HA: "That sounds nice Bill. Where will you go in your new car with your new clothes?"

Bill: "Wherever I want to. I have the money to go anywhere I want now."

HA: "I see... So, the money wasn't your purpose because as soon as you got it you began to get rid of it."

Bill: "Well yeah. Isn't the point of having money to spend it?"

HA: "Not in my book."

Bill: "Who doesn't want nice things?"

HA: "Nice things are great, but a purpose is greater. Novelty fades; purpose doesn't. How long do you think it will take before that new car is no longer new to you?"

Bill: "I can buy another one."

HA: "Then what will you do when that one begins to lose its luster?"

Bill: "I am beginning to see what you are saying."

HA: "That is a start."

Bill: "Then what should my purpose be?"

HA: "That is for you to discover. My assumption is,

your final destination is your true source of happiness. There you will find your purpose."

If you are where Bill is that is not the worst place you could be. You will have an issue however if you stay there. You can begin to F.E.A.R right now. Where would you go if you were not confined to a schedule dictated to you by your job or your current circumstances?

If everything was accessible to you, what would you change about yourself? What would you change about the world? Who would you spend time with? Where would you spend it? How would you spend it? Ponder and reflect on your answers; the correct choice will become obvious.

My purpose was presented to me and everything shifted. Like most people, the birth of a child is a life altering event and I am no different. I cannot say whether it is chemical or cosmic. I can say it was and is clear. My daughter has affected my views of myself and everything around us in innumerable ways.

Waking up knowing that someone else is counting on you to survive is a serious responsibility and a welcomed challenge. I found my destination. I found my copilot. Keeping her safe was and is my number one priority. With this new-found purpose all of my other choices became easy. Is this going to benefit or take away from her?

At times what was perceived to be the best decision in the moment may or may not have been what was best for her. As a parent that is something I have to work through. For all the parents reading this chapter you might relate to the idea that anytime your child feels pain, especially if you inflicted it, that somehow you could have done better. The truth is perhaps you could have; however, if you were doing so with their best intentions in mind, then you have to allow yourself room for correction.

I remember several years ago I would practice skip counting with my daughter in our car rides. She hated it. She needed the extra practice so I did anything I could to try and make it fun for her. Those attempts often fell flat. It was a tough pill to swallow.

To put it in context: remember, I was a math teacher. I literally got paid to do this with other people's children and they loved it. Students would kick and scream for the opportunities she dreaded and it did not make sense to me as a young father.

My baby girl didn't want a math teacher; she wanted a wrestling partner or a video game partner. Someone to draw with or build a fort with. We did all of those things (sometimes back to back to back to back to... you get it if you have children or if you have ever been around children).

. . .

NOTHING BROUGHT her more joy than thumb wrestling or playing in the park. All my little shadow wanted was a friend, someone to share ice cream concoctions loaded with cookies, chocolates, and candy with.

My little scientist was only looking for fun. As a child that's all we can hope for. The preservation of that innocence was and still is my purpose. My job daily is to ensure her life is as easy as possible even if she doesn't understand why we had to skip count. That doesn't make it easier but it did make the hard-parenting choices palatable.

One of my biggest mistakes as a parent was chasing money. I thought that money would equal security in terms of assuring my daughter's future was protected. I would work long hours and literally work seven (7) days a week.

My thought was that if I put in all of the time I can now, I would have plenty of time later. Luckily I found financial freedom in a few short years. Most people do not find this to be the case in their lives.

As fate would have it I was forced to slow down and in that process of halting I was able to focus on what was important. Quality time is more precious and valuable than any tangible item that I can think of. If you are working two or three jobs, maybe you're working full time and you're going to school or you're working on four different business ventures all simultaneously, my advice is to stop.

At my peak I remember calculating how many hours a week I actually spent with my daughter and it was sickening. We would drive up the block to her aunt's house at 7:00 am (five minutes) because I couldn't bring her to school due to my start time at work. Then I would pick her up from after school at 5:45 pm (ten minutes) because my work schedule didn't allow me to pick her up from school.

After my regular work schedule, I had tutoring sessions, meetings or personal training sessions that took place three to four (3-4) times a week. Then we would eat dinner, she would shower and before you know it was 7:30 pm and her bedtime was 8:00 pm. On Saturday's we would spend time together, usually a family day so I estimated 8 hours of time together (because naps were and still are essential to our survival).

Sunday's I would tutor and personally train clients all day. I would leave the house around 8:00am and arrive back home around 6:00pm for dinner. My estimate was 10 hours a week of time spent together. That was not enough. Something had to give. And it did.

I realized that I was spending so much time away from the person I was working for. What was the point? She was comfortable, her future was more secure than her counterparts and most adult Americans. Why was I missing the time I had with her? F.E.A.R kicked in. I had to evaluate my choices.

The car I was driving, the lifestyle, the ventures all had to be reassessed. If I had a $1,200 a month car bill and I was making $300 a day on a Sunday then if I got rid of my $1,200 bill I could give up my Sunday work. I also began investing more into real estate and my ventures that brought passive income.

The math became extremely simple. If I cut my car bill in half and I took that money and added it to investments that made money I could have more time to spend with my daughter. That's exactly what I did.

I subcontracted my tutoring sessions which allowed me to continue to earn income while not being in attendance. I spot checked at a set time to ensure the sessions were going according to plan and I gave up personal training. I used that time to focus on investing and spending quality time with my little baby bear.

If I had to do it all over again, I believe I would have made less luxury purchases and more investments. If we were to look at the benefits across a timeline, I would have been able to have the same luxury items and I would have been able to spend the quality time with my daughter. I wanted both in the same time span.

Fortunately for us I was able to figure it out in a few years. If you are younger than I was at the time or even if you are the same age or older, you must learn this lesson now if you are struggling with time management.

Delayed gratification pays more dividends than instant gratification. During the resetting period concerning my schedule and my priorities I had a discussion. The way things were going financially my goal was to get the BMW I was currently driving and within two years I would be driving the Bentley coupe I always wanted.

Check number one I got the BMW a year had passed and the Bentley coupe was on the horizon except it wasn't on my radar any longer, baby bear was, freedom was.

Somehow, I ended up in a conversation with someone whom I had known for a few years and had shared my vision with. This person was upper middle class. Between her and her husband (not including investments and alternate income), they made $300,000 a year. Not bad for a married couple in their 50s. They both worked 60-hour weeks for their primary careers and for a time their lifestyle seemed like a seemingly fitting one until my reset occurred.

They had a large home and expensive automobiles. Around the time I began to finance my new vehicle, she and her husband began to finance a new Jaguar. A year later it was time to finance another vehicle and thus the conversation arose.

It went something like this...

"How is the Bentley shopping going?"

HA: "I don't know. I don't think that's going to happen any time soon."

"Really? We are looking into getting a new Range Rover. We were looking at the new 4-door Porsche but it doesn't have a push button start so I think we are going to get a new truck."

HA: "I see. That sounds cool."

"Why aren't you thinking about buying your Bentley? Is everything alright with your business?"

HA: "Yeah, business is great. It's actually growing faster than I anticipated. I'm seeing how expensive this car I'm driving now is and I did some math."

"Oh, I get it. It's too expensive."

HA: "Something like that."

"Yeah, maybe in a few more years you will be able to afford it."

HA: "Actually, I could pay for it now but it doesn't make sense to park a $250,000 car outside of a school. Why would I spend all of that money to have a car I can't enjoy? My thoughts are if I continue to invest and drive a modest vehicle I can retire and actually enjoy my days."

*crickets

That conversation took place in 2016. I retired in 2019. The person I spoke to in that conversation and her husband are closing in on 60 and they still work 60-hour weeks for that same pay scale. At the time I am writing this chapter one of my companies grossed their salaries consecutively for the past four months of this year (it is July).

Outside of the COVID-19 pandemic I am able to take and pick my daughter up from her school. I travel several times a month and I can drive whatever car I want with no financial stress. I work 40-50 hours a week and I nap when I choose to. I did not inherit any significant lump sum or have any life altering financial stimulus outside of my shift in priorities and my purpose becoming clearer.

Once I understood what mattered the most was spending quality time with my daughter and having the freedom to do what I want when I wanted to, my thoughts and actions followed suit. Once I began to focus on what I enjoyed (which is still based in education) the days became more fruitful and everything fell into place.

I do not want to give the perception that I don't face challenges in my personal and my professional life, that is not the case. The takeaway is that when I face a trying circumstance, the obstacle isn't hard to deal with. I look at the state of affairs as an opportunity to grow.

When I was being paid a wage for my work, the motivation to excel was for the benefit of the students. If

I succeeded or failed my pay was still the same. That was a detractor. In business if I can solve a problem I am rewarded for it by helping clients, investors, and families on top of being compensated financially for my efforts.

The larger the task the larger the impact on the community as well as the financial benefits, which allow more freedom to spend quality time with Baby Bear; and, when it is all said and done, that is the purpose.

11

LOVE

If you love something, let it go. If it comes back to you, it's yours forever. If it doesn't, then it was never meant to be. "Unknown"

Ivy performing in
middle school
1989

Did you know that scientists and neurologists equate love to a series of neurons firing in the brain that produce a chemical called dopamine? That's it. No magic, no cosmic energy. Just dopamine: a feeling that can be duplicated by eating chocolate. I eat chocolate every day; I can say with 100% certainty, chocolate never made me feel so alive.

They say when you love someone
You just don't treat them bad
Oh and I feel so sad
Now that I want to leave
She's crying her heart to me
And I just need time to see
Where I wanna be
Where I want to be

If you know these lyrics and were born in the early to mid-1980s, you might have used these Donell Jones lyrics during your share of "it's not you, it's me" break up conversations.

Love is not easily describable. Love is one of those beautiful things in life that we just know. I knew I was in love at age six (6). I knew instantly, and I've never stopped knowing ever since. It was the fall of 1988.

The school year had just begun in September, as it always had in New York City. I began attending the first grade in elementary school, and my brother, who is my senior by six years, began his first days as a seventh grader at his middle school across the street from my building. Both schools were down the block from my grandmother's house.

We both met new teachers and classmates; some who lived close, others far away. My mother worked at the junior high school my brother attended at the time, so the conversations about school and the day were multilayered as my mother could offer different insights on things that a parent who didn't know the school as in depth could.

My mother knew everyone in the neighborhood. She lived there as a young adult. My family had been there for decades, and my mother had worked in the building for 12 years at that point. The name "Kemp" was well known in Park Slope in the 1990s and 2000s.

There was one name that came up that was a new one to me. This name would forever be etched in my brain and on my heart, "Ivy". And the first time I saw her, she became my "Winnie Cooper".

Ivy was the most beautiful girl in the world. She was 12 years old, and had long, straight, jet black hair that went all the way down her back. She had bangs and a smile that was electrifying. She lived around the corner from my grandmother's house. Her apartment was on the first floor.

Her mom would sit out the window, and that space was a common meeting ground that was known as "the corner". That meant I would get to see her almost every day. In fact, starting around the age of six (6), I would sit on my grandmother's stoop, and wait for her to walk up the block with her friends.

There was a rule that my mother and grandmother had that I couldn't go anywhere that wasn't visible. My mother didn't want me on the corner because there were always people there, and it was known for drug sales. My grandfather had a recliner that was positioned right next to the front window in the living room.

He always had a recliner; it was the best chair in the house. The area that I was allowed to travel to was clear. I could play in between the tree that was right in front of the house and the tree that was in front of the neighbor's house five doors down.

The stoop had bricks that acted as a barrier to separate the adjoining neighbor's property, and as a safety precaution for anyone who could misstep and fall into the basement entrance of the house. That brick barrier became a seat for most, and it was my post.

As soon as I saw her, I would run to the neighbor's tree and greet Ivy with a hug. I used to put my arm around her waist and she would let me walk her up to the next tree in front of my grandmother's house which was my final destination.

That was the highlight of my day. In speaking with her now, she told me she thought I was the cutest little boy. I thought we were married. She claims she was being nice but anyone reading this can see it was love at first sight (I am literally smiling while writing this). This pattern continued for some time. As the months and years would progress, Ivy would do like most teens and begin to show interest in other people.

I remember as I got a little older I was allowed more liberties including when I got my first bike. I was allowed to ride to Ivy's corner and back down the block all the way to 8th Avenue; that was huge. I used to spend way more time on the corner of 17th and 9th to get a glimpse of Ivy, and show her my new wheels.

There was one time I saw my arch nemesis Wayne Arnold (in keeping with the Wonder Years theme) talking to Ivy in front of her window. I was devastated. Now this was someone who always protected me and he was talking to my woman. He had to be dealt with expeditiously.

My brother was well known for being popular with the ladies. He wasn't going to steal my wife from me. We have to remember, I was around six or seven at the time. I thought hugging and holding hands was pretty much an engagement. I was smart. I knew kissing was being married.

I tried to move on and see other people but this was the woman of my dreams. This wouldn't be the last time that Ivy broke my young heart. Like before, some time would pass. Ivy had a new boyfriend. We are talking innocent teenage '90s kids stuff here.

Holding hands, walking up the block together with an arm around the shoulder, but in my 8 to 10-year-old mind this guy was going to have to be removed from the Earth immediately.

I remember intervening as often as I could. I believe Ivy had similar restrictions as most kids did (not my brother, this guy made his own rules). I knew where I could find Ivy and her new acquaintance, and I made sure I was there too. I would squeeze in between them. Interrupt conversations. Come around the corner; anything I could do. It wasn't enough. Then it happened...Wayne Arnold stepped in and saved the day.

My brother had a reputation for being a bit of a tough guy. His crew was known for stomping people out and other things. If you're from Brooklyn in the '80s and '90s you know exactly what I'm talking about when I say other things. If you don't know, don't worry about it.

Let me summarize my brother's junior high school career. He cut school and had so many fights that when it came time to graduate, they sent him to another junior high school in my neighborhood. I can continue, but his school career and teenage recollections are for his memoirs. We have already spent enough time talking about this Judas.

As fate would have it, Judas would have the chance to redeem himself. Ivy was a nice girl. She did well in school, she didn't run the streets so as one might suspect she befriended someone who was the same as her. A straight-laced young man. Well for whatever reason, it really didn't matter to me. My brother ended up getting in trouble with my mom for, I guess you would have to call it, bullying him.

When I got that news, the sky opened up. It meant I could do even more intervening and I was untouchable. I was a "made" guy now and Ivy hated my brother. I was basically Marlon Brando at this point, as my enemies were taking care of themselves. All I had to do was sit back and watch from my ivory tower.

The rest is a haze. When I was about eight or nine, my younger brother French and I would play truth or dare with the girls in his neighborhood. That led to truth or dare with the girls in my grandmother's neighborhood and so on.

By the time I was 10, I had taken a more serious interest in girls. I was traveling from Park Slope to Brighton Beach on my own. That was about a 45 minute to an hour bus ride. I had grown up a bit. By fifth grade, Ivy had become a memory. I do not remember seeing her any time after that ever again.

We move to the year 1994: I am a 12-year-old, ready for the seventh grade in junior high school and all the fun that comes along with it. I became my brother reincarnated in a sense. Just not as intense. I began to have my fights and collect my phone numbers. I got in trouble at school.

I was given the nickname "treinta" by the assistant principals because I was always in trouble in Spanish class, and I always had 30 minutes detention. It got so bad that I would show up to detention even when I didn't have it because I was so used to being there and that's where all my friends were.

There was one girl who ended up catching my attention in junior high school. She was a year older than me. We had the same friends from the same block. She actually lived on 17th and 9th too. She also happened to be Ivy's younger sister Mira. Aha!! I'm back in the game.

Now Ivy could see the new and improved Junior High School Kevin Arnold. I hadn't seen Ivy in a long time. I had a growth spurt, I slimmed down, my clothes got better. I had some jewelry. This was my shot.

I hung out with Ivy's sister almost every day. Not once ever did she mention her older sister. During that year or two not once ever did I see Ivy. I figured it out; Ivy had passed away. I had been to the corner, I had hung out with her sister for a duration of time, and never heard a word. We had mutual friends and her name was never brought up so logically I thought she died. That was the most rational thing to assume, wasn't it?

It became the truth for the next 20 years. Then one day I received a friend request on Facebook from Ivy something or other. I ignored it. I only knew two Ivy's in my life and both were deceased.

. . .

IF YOU USE Facebook you know that from time to time, you'll receive friend requests that are spam or a solicitation account. A few days went by and I was in bed bored to death so I went into my Facebook account and decided to clean out my inbox and other notifications.

I went through maybe 15 or so requests from random accounts, and from people I didn't want to associate with. Then I get to Ivy so and so, and like all the other requests, I open it and see what the page is about. I saw photographs of a gorgeous woman.

This account had too many photographs to be fake. It had family photographs and the same gorgeous woman over the years. I continued to explore the page and I noticed that we had over 50 mutual friends, including Ivy's younger sister Mira.

My heart instantly began to race. *Oh my God, they made an anniversary page for Ivy. They're commemorating her passing with a memorial page. It has her all grown up with kids and everything. Wait a minute, that is the dumbest thing you have ever thought Hussain, we are now all dumber for having read it, thank you.*

She wasn't dead. She had just been cheating on me for the last 25 years or so. Remember, we were married when I was 6, and I don't remember signing any divorce papers. The steps that took place over the next five seconds became very clear and executed with the precision of a brain surgeon; friend request accepted, send message, "Hi Ivy, how are you?"

Within seconds, she replied. Our conversation began to stagger as she was cleaning at the time. It was 10:00PM on a weekday and she was cleaning. As our texts continued, the responses became automatic.

From that moment on, I knew providence existed and we would no longer be separated; I must continue to remind you our tree walking nuptials took place in 1988 and we were married by the powers vested in me. We spoke via messenger almost the whole night. We also spoke almost the whole day following our late-night conversation.

During our conversation I told Ivy that I had a crush on her. Ivy told me that everyone who reaches out to her told her that and it usually led to messages being left or read as her interests were more focused on reminiscing not rekindling. In my case, I reminded her that I didn't reach out to her, she reached out to me. I also asked her what my name was.

I didn't think she knew it. She spelled it out almost instantly and said she only hesitated because she didn't want to misspell it. My confidence was off the charts. I was sold she wasn't seeing things as clearly as I was. In fact, I told her two things that changed her perspective from that moment on.

Friend Request Sent

2015

The first thing I told her following that I had a crush on her was that I thought she died. Now you might think, "Why on Earth would I tell her that?" My answer, "because I did (believe she was dead)."

She was taken aback and had the same response most of you have when reading that was my conclusion on her absence. She sent a million laughing emojis. She thought it was hilarious but she wasn't sold on the crush comment.

Then I shared one of the memories I had about her as a child and it was over. There was one night where Ivy took part in a school performance. I usually attended the performances because my mom volunteered or took part in the shows.

Ivy was a dancer and still is. On this night I was heartbroken over her. I forget exactly what caused this rush of emotions at such a young age, however the memory of the night I had was vivid.

I laid in bed with the lights off in my room. My brother wasn't home or else I probably would have gotten beat up for touching his stereo and tapes. This was also huge because I was afraid of the dark at that age. I laid in the bed thinking about Ivy as I listened to 1980s freestyle. Specifically, "Show Me" by the Cover Girls. Yup that's right, good old 1980s freestyle.

Show me, Show me, you really love me
Actions speak louder than words
Show me, Show me, you really need me
Cause all those lies I've already heard
Show me, Show me, you really love me
Let me believe that it's true
Show me, Show me, you really need me
And I'll get together with you

If you don't know the song, Google it and enjoy. She not only laughed at the song, she googled it, and the years and dates all lined up. She knew that I couldn't have made that up. Our conversation drifted into the '80s and the stories I shared with you in the previous paragraphs amongst others.

We often speak about how many things had to line up for that scenario to take place. Ivy was not really a social media person. I was and still am not really a person who shares my life on social media. She lived in another state. I thought she was dead.

There wasn't even a thought of her being someone to search for. A month prior or after, and we would have missed one another. At the time, Mind Molders was beginning to take off and Shape Bingo was picking up steam. Another new piece of my life was physical fitness.

One of my best friends, someone I call brother, Hal, took me under his wing and literally shaped my life as I know it today. As time went on, Ivy shared how I received a friend request. Typically, women do not request men on social media; it usually sends the wrong message.

Ivy has never requested a male on Facebook before that request and made it clear that if I had sent her a request and the same conversation took place, she wouldn't have given anything I said any real thought because it would have seemed as if the request was only sent to try and shoot my shot.

I used, and still use, social media for business purposes. I never put any private photographs, birthdays, or anything personal on my platforms. My Facebook page was no different. However, at the time I was helping Hal grow his fitness business so I promoted my progress photos and some clips from the gym on my page. While this promotion was taking place, I was also promoting my tutoring business.

I sent friend requests to all sorts of people and shared my page to gain attention. As it turns out, Mira shared my personal page with her sister and from what I was told by Ivy said, "you gotta see Yusef's little brother" (exactly why I wasn't sure she knew my name).

She went on to tell Ivy about my success in business and how good I was doing. Ivy said as soon as she saw my profile pic, in her words, "friend request sent". The alignment of all these things make this story even more compelling.

The final part of the puzzle was that Ivy's family moved to central Texas. My younger brother French was also living in central Texas, and as I mentioned earlier, the reason I began investing in Texas. He told me the benefits of investing in the city that Ivy's family was living in. I shared this information with Ivy, and she told me she had plans on moving back to that city in the near future. F.E.A.R took over and if I didn't believe in destiny before, I did now.

I have always been a risk taker. I am the type of person that is comfortable with learning as I am going. I am also the type of person that knows what I want, and I will work tirelessly until I achieve my goal.

The shift in my mindset after all of the things I had experienced previously had taught me to capitalize on an opportunity when it was presented. Too often we miss out on opportunities because of a variety of reasons.

Once Ivy became an option, she was the only option and has been ever since. She is my alpha and omega. She was my Winnie Cooper, Kelly Kapowski, and now she is my Gina Payne, the aunt Vivian to my uncle Phil.

Latidos - Puerto Rico
2019

12

CONCLUSION

Earlier in the book, I posed the question: is it better to have had love and lost it than to have never had love at all? The poetic answer is yes of course. Love is the most beautiful thing in the world, it's what makes life worth living. What if that isn't the case?

What if the unknown is better left a mystery? In mathematics, a rule can only exist when there are no cases that can be presented in opposition to your line of thought. The Pythagorean Theorem works in every instance.

It's simple logic. If I know "A" and I know "B" but I don't know "C", I can use that information to figure out the unknown if I find the sum of the squares of both A and B and then I take that value and take the square root of it.

In simple division when your denominator is "o" your answer is undefined because you cannot evenly divide items into zero groups. If you say it out loud it doesn't even sound good to hear.

Maybe the concept of having something and losing it, isn't worth the pursuit. When asked, heroin addicts typically say they are chasing the euphoric feelings of the first hit. When they describe the sensation and everything else surrounding the few moments of that high, it seems obvious by their actions that it's worth losing everything else just to get back to that space. With the knowledge of the possibility of having the best feeling known to man based on countless numbers of testimonies, would you try heroin?

Another immeasurable joy of life is parenthood. Sometimes parents undergo what some might categorize as the worst feeling known to humankind, the death of a child. If you have lost a child, you have my deepest condolences and my heart goes out to you. I cannot speak on this circumstance from personal experience. I can speak on behalf of friends and family who have, and do live with this loss daily.

My bet is if you asked them if they feel better now after their loss you wouldn't get an overwhelming majority of them saying their pain was worth their loss. My assumption is that if you proposed a scenario where they knew the outcome of their child's life span, a large segment of the group would admit to wishing their child was never born in the first place.

When you are raised in poverty you don't know anything else. You have nothing to compare your life-style to. Your daily interactions are just chalked up as normal. Not ideal, not easy, but tolerable. When you don't know what you don't know, ignorance is bliss.

Now on the flip side, if you take someone who was born into wealth and strip them of it, you could break someone's spirit. Imagine only knowing a life filled with luxury and the finest of all things. At the blink of an eye, it's all gone.

Like mathematical logic, if there are instances where the concept doesn't apply, then you do not have a rule. Am I saying don't pursue love (actually I am)? You shouldn't pursue love. Love should happen naturally. I'm not trying to convince you that love is bad. I'm also not trying to talk you out of procreating or pursuing wealth.

The thread of this book is the theory that you can achieve your aims in life with the proper mindset. In each story I shared with you throughout this book, I had a turning point or a wakeup call. The realizations I have experienced over the years have served as reminders that with the proper outlook on a state of affairs, you can come out on the other side better off than expected using conventional approaches to your condition.

Forgetting everything and resetting isn't the answer to all of your problems, just as a hammer isn't the right instrument for every repair. That doesn't make a hammer less useful. When required, having a hammer is the only way to get a job done, and on the same note, forgetting everything and resetting can serve you as a valuable tool for your success. The utilization of this technique can optimize your opportunities, if used correctly.

As I am writing this book, my country is at civil unrest. The murder of George Floyd has led to protests and riots in cities all across the states, that, coupled with the COVID-19 pandemic and the new norms surrounding social distancing, has America on edge.

Poor leadership, an increase in unemployment and poverty, on top of the resurgence of outright racism and bigotry in this society, have us at a boiling point. The masses could use F.E.A.R right now. We can all collectively use a deep breath, and a fresh look at what we are facing.

F.E.A.R isn't about forgiving and forgetting. It is about taking a step back and reassessing. Sometimes when you're in the fight, you can't see what an outsider can see. At times, we can all be blinded by our motivations, biases, and emotions. The key is not to let these factors control the outcome of what we are encountering.

By starting over and taking an appraisal, perhaps you can find common ground and use those as building blocks towards a solution to a problem. In other cases, you can clearly define your issue, and unequivocally determine it is time to remove yourself from the situation.

I thank you and I hope that you have positive takeaways from this book. I hope that you find success now and moving forward.

ABOUT THE AUTHOR

Hussain Abdullah was born in Brooklyn, New York. At a young age, he learned that if he invested in himself or a product, he would reap the benefits of his efforts. Growing up, he always had a knack for creating different opportunities to generate income, even as early as age six (6).

He was first introduced to real estate investments in 2000 and closed on his first investment property less than four years later. He used his knowledge of numbers in formal education as a math teacher and staff developer for New York City Department of Education (NYCDOE) in which he worked for over a 14 year career to garner a profession he could be proud of. All of these choices allowed him to retire in 2019 at the age of 37.

The thought of writing a book never occurred to him; however, friends and family encouraged him to compile some of his philosophies and expertise in a way that is accessible for people who may not have the resources to begin real estate investments.

One Saturday morning, he started typing out a memory from his life that he felt was a great example of how misconceptions about investing could hinder someone from becoming a potential investor. That one note turned into more Saturday morning chronicles and he soon had enough material to consider publishing a book. "F.E.A.R." was then activated, and in November 2020, was released as his debut self-empowerment book.

Hussain Abdullah currently owns and invests in several companies, including real estate, consulting, and education. He tours nationwide, conducting presentations and workshops for all ages and walks of life. With a primary focus of reinvesting in the communities,

Hussain's goal is to give back and encourage potential investors to pursue happiness and to know their dreams are achievable.

Connect with Hussain and learn about his businesses by searching **HAHOMESUS** on the following platforms:

INDEX